This Text Book is useful for Sir Parashurambhau College of Arts, Science and Commerce, Pune. (Autonomous)

Economics (G-3)

Economics of Development and Growth - I

T.Y. B. A. (Sem. - V) (Course Code : EC3516)

Dr. Hemlata Namdev Kavare
Asst. Professor
(MA, M.Phil, Ph.D. Economics)
Shikshana Prasaraka Mandali's Sir Parashurambhau College, Pune.

❖❖❖❖❖❖❖❖❖❖❖❖

2023

Price: 100/-

SUCCESS PUBLICATIONS

Published by
Dr. Rajesh M. Patne
Success Publications
Radha Krishna Apartment, 535, Shaniwar Peth,
Appa Balwant Chowk, Opp. Prabhat Talkies, Pune - 411 030.
Ph. 24434662 Mobile : 9325315464.

Copyrights
With the Publishers

Printed at
Success Publications
S. No. 30/27, Laxmi Industrial Estate,
Near Prabhat News Paper, Dhayari, Pune-41.

Edition
2023

Edited By
Mr. Valmik Gaikwad

Typesetting, Layout
Mr. Valmik Gaikwad

Cover Designing
Miss. Varsha Lokhande

Preface

It is a matter of great pleasure for us to present this book to our esteemed readers. This book has been designed as standard text on 'Economics of Development and Growth–I' for T.Y.B.A. (Sem. -V).

This book comprehensively covers the entire syllabus of T.Y.B.A. (Sem. - V) Course of Sir Parashurambhau College (Autonomous), Pune effective from 2021 onwards. It has been written to meet the requirements of students of T.Y.B.A. (Sem. - V) Some of the special features of the book are as follows:

1. *Full coverage of the revised syllabus of T.Y.B.A. (Sem. - V).*
2. *Chapter outline at the beginning of each chapter to give a bird's eye view of the topics covered in the chapter.*
3. *Point wise explanation of each topic in the chapter.*
4. *Topics are logically arranged in numbered paragraphs exactly according to the modified syllabus.*
5. *Proposed questions at the end of each chapter.*
6. *Extensive use of diagrams, tables and various forms to give visual view of key concepts and techniques.*
7. *Conversational, lucid and simple language.*

Every effort has been made to provide the readers with most up-to-date and authentic material on the subject.

We are very grateful to our publisher Mrs. and Mr. Rajesh Patne who have rendered all possible assistance in bringing out this book. We wish to acknowledge our deep gratitude to staff who have assisted and helped us in preparing this book. We will consider our efforts amply rewarded in case the book proves useful to the students and teachers of the subject.

Suggestions of readers are welcome and shall be acknowledged with gratitude.

With best wishes.

By Authors

Syllabus

T. Y. B.A. (Sem. - V)

Economics G-3 (Economics of Development and Growth - I)

(Course Code – EC3516)

Unit No.	Unit Title & Contents	No. of Lectures
1	**Economic Development and Growth**	**12**
	• Meaning of Economic Development and Growth • Indicators of Economic Growth • Indicators of Economic Development • Differences between Economic Development & Growth	
2	**Developed and Developing Countries**	**10**
	• Concept- Developed, Developing Countries • Characteristics of Developing Countries • Economic Characteristics • Demographic Characteristics • Technological Characteristics • Socio – Cultural Characteristics • Other Characteristics	
3	**Constraints to Development Process**	**16**
	• Vicious Circle of Poverty • Population Explosion • Low Productivity of Agriculture • Scarcity of Capital • Inappropriate Technology • Socio- Cultural Constraints • Political and Administrative Constraints • External Bottleneck	
4	**Theories of Economic Development**	**10**
	• Classical Theories- Adam Smith, Ricardo & Malthus • Karl Mark's Theory of Economic Development • Schumpeterian Theory of Economic Development	
	Total	**48**

INDEX

T. Y. B.A. (Sem. - V)

Economics G-3 (Economics of Development and Growth - I)

(Course Code – EC3516)

Economic Development and Growth

UNIT 1

Introduction:

Growth and Development are importance factors of Economics.Economic development ideally refers to the sustained, concerted actions of communities and policymakers that improve the standard of living and economic health of a specific locality. The definition of economic development given by Professor Michael Tovar is an increase in living conditions, improvement of the citizens self-esteem needs and free and a just society. He suggests that the most accurate method of measuring economic development is the Human Development Index which takes into account the literacy rates & life expectancy which in-turn has an outright impact on productivity and could lead to Economic Growth. However, economic development can also be measured by taking into account the GDI (gender related index). Economic development can also be referred to as the quantitative and qualitative changes in an existing economy. Economic development involves development of human capital, increasing the literacy ratio, improve important infrastructure, improvement of health and safety and others areas that aims at increasing the general welfare of the citizens. The terms economic development and economic growth are used interchangeably but there is a very big difference between the two. Economic growth can be viewed as a sub category of economic development. Economic development is a government policy to increase the economic, social welfare and ensuring a stable political environment. Economic growth on the other hand is the general increase in the country products and services output.

1.1 Economic Development:

Economic development, in contrast to economic growth, is a wider concept. It is a complex term. To give it a precise definition is not easy. Development, as we know, is defined as economic development plus social change. Social change consists of better living standards for people, equitable distribution of income and wealth, productive employment facilities for all, adequate facilities for health and sanitation, education for everyone etc. These are reflected in social indicators like life expectancy at birth, literacy rate, birth rate and death rate per 1,000 population, hospitals per 100,000 population, schools per 100,000 populations, share of labour force employed in agriculture sector etc. Attempts to define development have led to some general definitions. Many of them differ from one another, particularly in respect of substance and the index of development. The key element of development is that people are the major participants in the process of change in the economy as well as in the enjoyment of benefits flowing from these changes. This process of change in the economy is what is referred to as economic development. These factors enhance growth of the economy though in an indirect way. The enjoyment of benefits by all could be referred to as development. Basically, economic development implies the process of securing higher and higher levels of production in all sectors of the economy and this, in turn, is a function of the level of technology.

1.2.1 Meaning:

Economic development is a process whereby an economy's real national income as well as per capita income increases over a long period of time. Here, the process implies the impact of certain forces which operate over a long period and embody changes in dynamic elements. It contains changes in resource supplies, in the rate of capital formation, in demographic composition, in technology, skills and efficiency, in institutional and organisational set-up. It also implies respective changes in the structure of demand for goods, in the level and pattern of income distribution, in size and composition of population, in consumption habits and living standards and in the pattern of social relationships and religious dogmas, ideas and institutions. In short, economic development is a process consisting of a long chain of inter-related changes in fundamental factors of supply and in the structure of demand, leading to a rise in the net national product of a country in the long run.

1.2.2 Definitions:

Following are the definitions of the economic development:

1) **Simple Definition:**

   "It refers to the process whereby the total supply of goods and services of the society increases leading towards improved living standard."

2) **Michael P. Tovar:**

   "Development must be conceived (considered) for as a multi-dimensional process involving major change in social structures, popular attitudes and national institutions as well as the acceleration of eco-growth, the eradication (end) of poverty and reduction of inequality of wealth."

3) **Prof. Meier and Baldwin:**
   "Economic development is a process whereby an economy's real national income increases over a long period of time".
4) **BenardOkun and Richard W, Richardson:**
   "Economic development may be defined as a sustained secular improvement in well-being, which may be considered to be reflected in an increasing flow of goods and services".

1.2.3 Indicators of Economic Development:

There is misunderstanding among the economists over the indicators of economic development. Some of the economists have taken national product as the indicator of economic development. Some other economists have taken per capita income as the indicator of economic development. Likewise some other economists have taken economic welfare as the indicator of economic development. Various economists have taken material living standard index as the indicator of economic development. Economists of this thought have taken life-span, death rate, literacy rate as the bases. Similarly United Nations Development Program (UNDP) has developed Human Development Index (HDI) as the indicator of economic development. The indicators are income, literacy and life expectancy. The pointed of indicators lies between 0 and 1.The position up to 0.5 is the lower class of human development. From 0.5 to 0.8 is the middle class and above 0.8 is the upper class. The base of economic development indicators are as follows.

1) **High Real National Income:**
   High national income is a common indicator of economic development, accepted by most of the economists. Usually, high national income indicates high level of economic development. High real national income of a country is the index of higher economic development. The real national income is the measuring rod of economic development. The word 'real' signifies purchasing power. If the national income increases, prices remain the same then real national income increases. A developed economy generates more income so it is considered as the indicator of development.
2) **Increase in Welfare of the People:**
   Economic well-being of the people depends upon the availability of sufficient goods and services. If the production increases substantially then people can satisfy their all types of wants easily. Thus, increase in the economic welfare of people, is the indicator of Economic Development.
3) **Technical Changes:**
   Economic development indicates more output and more welfare. It is possible due to technical progress. Economic development implies changes in the technical and

institutional arrangement by which more goods are produced. So the ways and means for raising the national income i.e. technology indicates economic development.

4) Efficient Use of Resources:

Economic development refers to the process whereby people utilise the resources. So, optimum utilisation and minimizing wastes indicates economic development.

5) Removal of Poverty and Inequality of Income:

The underdeveloped countries are caught in the vicious circle of poverty. They have wide inequalities of income also. As the economy develops employment, income, etc. increases. In the course of time absolute poverty is eradicated. As the employment opportunities increase, income inequalities reduce. Reduction in poverty and unemployment indicate economic development.

6) High Quality of Human Resource:

High quality of population is indicated by high life expectancy, high standard of health, development of work-culture, scientific attitude among the people, etc. This is the result of economic progress or development. Quality of population and that of human life indicates economic development. In a developed economy people live a good life and have self-esteem. In the less developed economies, people suffer from miseries, have traditional attitude and are lazy. As the economy develops the above mentioned changes take place.

7) Development of Agriculture:

High agricultural productivity and developed agriculture makes the country self-sufficient in food grains, cash crops, etc. Economic development revolutionises agriculture. So, developed agriculture indicates economic development.

8) Industrialisation:

Industrialisation of the economy is considered as a key to economic development. Developments of the basic and key industries that are capital goods industries indicate economic development. Industries producing consumer goods satisfy different types of needs of the people. New job opportunities are created. So income and standard of living of the people improves. This is an indicator of economic development.

9) Favourable Terms of Trade:

Terms of trade refers to the external position of a country. Favourable terms of trade how excess of foreign exchange earnings over the payments. This is one of the desirable balance of payments positions which are in many cases, the indicator of economic development.

10) Increase in the Government's Revenue:

Economic development increases the level of national output and per capita income. So taxpaying capacity of the people increases and the government can collect larger revenues by way of taxes. The increased tax revenue leads to the fiscal reliance of the government. This is an indicator of economic development as the government of a less developed country usually faces fiscal deficit.

11) Social Security:

If the government is looking after old, handicapped person and also the unemployed and poor, then such social security measures adopted by the government, indicate economic development.

12) Import Substitution:

It is the sign of economic development. The improved techniques of production, use of new machinery make it possible. As the number of substitute products goes on increasing, unnecessary dependence on imports can be avoided. Such a country slowly becomes 'self-reliant'. Import substitution makes possible savings of foreign exchange reserves. Budgetary provisions for research and development activities in the country make possible to develop new products, which are the 'real substitutes' for imported goods. Import substitution also makes possible to avoid competition by foreign companies in Indian markets.

1.2.4 Need of Economic Development:

Economic development is a critical component that drives economic growth in our economy, creating high wage jobs and facilitating an improved quality of life. The business development team at the Orlando Economic Partnership works to attract, and retain jobs for the Orlando region. While the work of economic developers often falls under the radar, creating and sustaining jobs for a region is a critical component to a successful economy and community. Need of economic development explained with following points:

1) Job Creation:

Economic developers provide critical assistance and information to companies that create jobs in our economy. We help to connect new-to-market and existing companies with the resources and partners they need to expand, such as Career Source Central Florida, utilities, and county and city partners.

2) Industry Diversification:

A core part of economic development works to diversify the economy, reducing a region's vulnerability to a single industry. While tourism plays an important role in creating jobs in the Orlando region, economic development efforts help to grow industries outside of tourism, including Innovative Technologies and Digital Media, Life Sciences & Healthcare, Aviation, Aerospace & Defense, Advanced Manufacturing, and Business Services.

3) Business Retention and Expansion:

A large percentage of jobs in the Orlando economy are created by existing companies that are expanding their operations. Our economic development team executed 73 business retention and expansion visits to local companies just last year to assist with their operational needs.

4) **Economy Fortification:**
Economic development helps to protect the local economy from economic downturns by attracting and expanding the region's major employers.

5) **Increased Tax Revenue:**
The increased presence of companies in the region translates to increased tax revenue for community projects and local infrastructure.

6) **Improved Quality of Life:**
Better infrastructure and more jobs improve the economy of the region and raise the standard of living for its residents.

1.2.5 Importance of Economic Development:

There are various benefits which accrue to the less developed countries through economic development.

1) **Capital Formation:**
There can be no two opinions about the fact that economic development depends upon capital formation. But it is also true that economic development helps in the formation of capital. Economic development helps in raising the productivity of agriculture, industry and thereby creating economic surplus. The economic surplus can be used for productive and development activities which in turn raises income, saving and capital formation. Thus development and capital formation are mutually reinforcing.

2) **Exploitation of Natural Resources:**
Economic development promotes scientific knowledge and technology, which in turn helps in the invention of new instruments, new apparatuses and techniques for the exploitation and preservation of natural resources. Once the natural resources are fully and judiciously exploited, many other benefits start accruing in the shape of improved irrigation al facilities, generation of electricity, expansion of mineral wealth, etc. As a matter of fact, economic development changes the complexion of the entire economy and progress takes the place of stagnation. It can be justifiably said that economic development provides mechanism for the exploration, exploitation and utilisation of natural resources.

3) **Development of Agriculture:**
The backwardness of agriculture is an important feature of the underdeveloped countries. Economic development not only helps in removing the backwardness, but also acts as an instrument for self-reliance. In the past, agriculture was considered as a means of subsistence but now it can be made a profitable occupation by increasing its productivity through the application of new methods of production, new

techniques and new experiments. The study of economic development throws light on the new techniques and new methods. Actually, these are the boons of economic development. In India, the green revolution has been accomplished through the instrument of economic development. It would suffice to say that economic development revolutionises agriculture.

4) **Development of Industries:**

Development of industries is another gift of economic development. It is an admitted fact that agriculture and industry are complementary to each other. The development of these two sectors is inter-dependent. The developed agricultural sector helps in rapid industrialisation. Necessary raw material is provided by agriculture for the growth of industries. New industries are set up and with them numerous subsidiary industries also spring up. In this way process of industrialisation gets momentum. Moreover, employment opportunities are created, which tend to reduce unemployment. Industrialisation meets the diverse needs of the masses, thereby creating an environment of satisfaction among the people. In brief we can say that economic development sows the seeds of industrialisation.

5) **Increase in National Output:**

Economic development helps in raising the agricultural and industrial productivity of a country. The expansion of these two sectors contributes in raising the level of national output. Higher income offers the ability to choose. People can have more things and can diminish their hunger, disease and early death. But it must be remembered that increase in national output can be meaningful only if population of the country is kept under check. Otherwise, the growth of population will eat away the cake of national output. This type of situation will lead the country to the state of privation and hopelessness. So efforts must be made to control and check the growth of population so that masses may relish the sweet fruits of economic development.

6) **Expansion of Social Services:**

Another important gift of economic development is the expansion of social services (i.e. education, health services, roads, means of communications, electricity, etc.). As development precedes the demand for social services and the expansion of existing services arises. To cope with the rising demand for the expansion of social services, state governments attempt to make larger investment allocation for the purpose. This way the expansion of social services becomes a corollary of development. These services help in removing illiteracy, privation, poverty, disease etc. Expansion of social services ushers an era of plenty and self-reliance, such an environment creates a sense of confidence in the minds of the masses and their thinking becomes development oriented. So, expansion of social services can be considered as a special benefit of economic development.

7) International Status:

As development proceeds, the public aspirations grow high. The demand for higher wages arises and that can be met by raising the levels of development tempo. This is possible through technological development. Countries grow richer with technological development and economic growth and thereby acquire esteem and recognition in the comity of nations. The countries of the first world (U.S.A., Canada, U.K.) have gained international esteem because of their better performance in development arena.

8) Take off:

The underdeveloped countries are more interested in achieving the stage of "take off" as early as possible. This task can be accomplished through the instrument of economic development. All the essential conditions of the "Take off" can be met by the accelerated pace of economic development, so economic development has a special message for the governments of underdeveloped countries, as the ultimate end of economic development is self-reliance.

9) Increase in Public Revenue:

It has already been pointed out that economic development raises the level of national output and the per capita income of the masses. Higher per capita income enhances the taxable capacity of the people. The government can collect larger revenues by exploiting higher taxable capacity of the people. This way, government can achieve the objective of fiscal reliance and can carry on various development activities to promote national welfare. Another bright feature of fiscal self-reliance is that country will not be required to depend upon external aid or foreign assistance. Foreign capital import can be dispensed with when large development endeavour is made at home.

10) Social Significance:

So far we have discussed the economic importance of development and now we touch upon its social significance. Economic development exerts a greater control over the environment and thus increases the range of human choice. Though it may not necessarily result in greater human happiness. It increases freedom as the effort in relation to output is reduced. Less work would be required to satisfy human wants and greater leisure would be available for fostering higher values of life. Nature is often harsh and niggardly subjecting human life to disease and scarcity of essential things. The important contribution that economic growth can make is to free life from the menace of nature.

1.2 Economic Growth:

A startling fact about economic growth is the large variation in the growth experience of different countries in recent history. Some parts of the world, like the United States or Western Europe, experienced sustained economic growth over a period of more than

100 years, so by historical standards these countries are now enormously wealthy. This is not only true in absolute terms (i.e., GDP), but also if we measure wealth as income per capita (i.e., GDP per person). In contrast, there are countries where even today large parts of the population live close to the subsistence level, much the same as Europeans and Americans did some hundreds of years ago. Also, a group of countries that used to be relatively poor around the time of World War II managed to achieve even higher growth rates than the western industrialized countries, so their per capita incomes now approach those of western countries

1.2.1 Meaning:

Economic growth is the increase in the inflation-adjusted market value of the goods and services produced by an economy over time. It is conventionally measured as the percent rate of increase in real gross domestic product, or real GDP. Of more importance is the growth of the ratio of GDP to population (GDP per capita, which is also called per capita income). An increase in growth caused by more efficient use of inputs (such as physical capital, population, or territory) is referred to as intensive growth. GDP growth caused only by increases in the amount of inputs available for use is called extensive growth.

1.2.2 Definitions:

Following are the definitions of economic growth:

1) *"A simple definition is that it is an increase in the level of output of goods and services that is sustained over a long period of time, measured in terms of value added."*
2) **Michael P. Tovar:**

   "Economic growth is a steady process by which the productive capacity of the economy is increased over time to bring about rising levels of national output and income".
3) **Simon Kuznets:**

   "Economic growth may be defined as a long term process wherein the substantial and sustained rise in real national income, total population and real per capita income takes place".

1.2.3 Indicators of Economic Growth:

An economic growth is the indicated by increase in capital resources, improvement in efficiency of labour, better organisation of production in all spheres, development of means of transport and communication, growth of banks and other financial institutions, urbanisation and a rise in the level of living, improvement in the standards of education and expectation of life, greater leisure and more recreation facilities and the widening of the mental horizon of the people and so on. In short, economic development must break the poverty barrier or the vicious circle and bring into being a self-generating economy so that economic growth becomes self-sustained.

1) Significance of Industrial Sector

Most of the developed countries in the world have given much importance of the growth of industrial sector. They have large capacities to utilise all resources of production, to maximise national income and to provide employment for the jobless people. These countries receive the major portion of their national income from the non-agriculture sectors which include industry, trade, transport and communication. For instance, England generally receives nearly 50% of her national income from industrial sector, 21% from transport and commerce, 4% from agriculture and 25% from other sectors. The same case is with the U.S.A., Japan and other West European countries. But in India and other developing countries agriculture contributes, say, 35 to 40 percent, to their national income.

2) High Rate of Capital Formation:

Grown countries are generally very rich as they maintain a high level of savings and investment, with the result that they have huge amount of capital stocks. The rate of investment constitutes 20 to 25 percent of the total national income. The rate of capital formation in these countries is also very high. Besides this, well-developed capital markets, high level of savings, broader business prospects and capable entrepreneurship have led to a high growth of capital formation in these economies.

3) Use of High Production Techniques and Skills:

High production techniques and skills have become an essential part of economic growth process in the developed countries. The new techniques have been used for the exploitation of the physical human resources. These countries have, therefore, been giving priority to the scientific research, so as to improve and evolve the new and technique of production. Consequently, these countries find themselves able to produce goods and services of a better equality comparatively at the lesser cost. It is because of the use of high production techniques and latest skills, that the countries like Japan, Germany and Israel could have developed their economies very rapidly, though they have limited natural resources.

4) Low Growth of Population:

The developed countries, like the U.S.A., the U.K. and other Western European countries have low growth of population because they have low level of birth rate followed by low level of death rate. Good health conditions, high degree of education and high level of consumption of the people have led to maintain low growth of population followed by low level of birth and death rates. The life expectancy in these countries is also very high. The high rate of capital formation on the one hand and low growth of population have resulted in high level of per capita income and prosperity in these countries. Consequently, the people in these countries enjoy a higher standard of living and work together unitedly for more rapid economic and industrial development of the nations. Besides this, the entire society, its structure and values are found to be dedicated to the goal of rapid economic and industrial development. The position of individuals in the society is decided by the ability of the persons and not by their birth, caste or creed. Dignity of labour is maintained. The economic motive and strong desire to lead a better social life always inspire people to contribute to the process of development. The main objective of rapid economic development, particularly in the developed economies is to achieve the level of stagnant economic growth, so that they may maintain the existing economic status and exercise control over business cycle.

5) **Low Level of Poverty:**

This subcategory covers income distribution and poverty. Poverty is measured nationally and separately as a percentage of rural population and urban populations. Income distribution is measured by quintiles and deciles. A heading called "Conflict and Fragility" measures battle-related deaths and homicides.

1.2.4 Difference between Economic Growth & Economic Development:

Both the terms seem similar, but there are various following points, which create difference between these two:

Economic Growth	Economic Development
1- Definition	
The term economic growth is only concerned with raising income level and volume of production of goods and services.	The basic feature of economic development is to raise income level and improve the human being.
2- Nature in Economic Literature	
Economic growth is the key issue under traditional economics. According to this approach "take care of growth and poverty would eliminate automatically."	Economic development is the main issue under modern economics literature. Accordingly, "take care of poverty and growth would take care of itself."
3- Scope	
Scope of economic growth is narrow because it is concerned with changes in income level only.	Scope of economic development is wide and comprehensive than economic growth. Its link is not only with income but also with the prosperity of the society and economy.
4- Institutional changes	
In case of economic growth strong and effective institutional set-up is not	Efficient institutional set-up is necessary. Effective and strong institutional

necessary.	revolution is the sign of economic development.
5- Type of Approach	
According to various economists, economic growth is said to be quantitative approach.	Economic development refers to the qualitative approach.
6- Importance	
Economic growth is less important due to the attachment with income level only.	The Concept of economic development is more important because it discusses an economy in wider sense.
7- Time Span	
Economic growth is a short-term process. We can measure income changes yearly. So, its time span may be of one year.	Economic development is a long-term process about 20 to 25 years. Because it takes years to change social, economic and institutional set-up.
8- National Problem	
Economic growth is the problem of developed countries of the world.	Economic development is the problem of developing countries.
9- Political Changes	
Economic growth is not concerned with the political stability.	The concept of economic development is incomplete without political stability.
10- Dependence and Self-Sufficiency	
Economic growth does not ensure the freedom from the dependence of foreign countries.	In case of economic development our dependence on other countries reduces and country adopts the self-reliance policy.
11- Economic Application	
Economic growth first checks the statistical upward movement in the economy.	Economic development basically emphasizes on the balanced growth of economy.
12- Social Impact	
There may or may not be any social changes in case of economic growth. It ignores the human beings and it is only concerned with income level etc.	Social changes, in case of economic development, are compulsory. It refers to the better jobs, availability of food, better health and education etc.
13- Economic Welfare	
Economic growth is not much attached	In economic development, more

with the human beings. It has no link with the good or bad.	importance is given to the mankind as compare to the economic growth.
14- Measurement	
Economic growth is measured only by comparing income levels of different years. It also can be measured numerically.	Measurement of economic development is based on the reduction in poverty, development of human being and living standard etc.

❖❖❖❖❖❖❖❖

Review Questions

Q. 1. Answer in 100 Words:

1) State the Concept of Economic Development.
2) Explain the Concept of Economic Growth.

Q. 2. Answer in 200 Words:

1) Explain in detail Need of Economic Development.
2) Discuss the Importance of Economic Development.
3) Explain the Indicators of Economic Growth.
4) State the differences between Economic Growth & Development.

Q. 3. Answer in 300 Words:

1) What is Economic Development? Explain the Indicators of Economic Development.
2) Define Economic Development. State the Need and Importance of Economic Development.
3) What is Economic Growth? Explain the Indicators of Economic Growth.

Q.4 Write Short Note on Following:

1) Meaning of Economic Development.
2) Meaning of Economic Growth.
3) Indicators of Economic Development.
4) Indicators of Economic Growth.

❖❖❖❖❖❖❖❖

Developed and Developing Countries

UNIT 2

2.1 Developed Countries
2.2 Developing Countries

Introduction:

Developing countries depend on the developed countries for help to establish their industries. They have only begun to taste the growth of the economy. Developing countries are in the beginning stages of development in the areas of education, business, and transportation. Developing countries are characterized by many shortcomings. These shortcomings include less awareness regarding matters relating to health, poor amenities, shortage in water supply, shortcoming in the area of medical supply, a higher rate of birth rate. The most important and worrying factor in the developing countries is the factor of poor nutrition. Poor nutrition to both mothers and infants is the main concern in the developing countries. Due to high birth rates, the probability of natural diseases is more in developing countries. Hence, the death rates are also eventually high in developing countries. Since natural diseases increase by high rates in the developing countries, they will have a short population doubling time. In the case of developing countries, there is usually a big gap between the birth rate and the death rate. Infant mortality factor is influenced by the development factor of countries. A developing country for that matter would have higher infant mortality than a developed country.

2.1. Developed Countries:

The size of the progress of a country can be seen from the successful development of the country. Income per capita, economic growth, unemployment and population growth rate is partly an indicator to measure the success of development. Grouping the countries into developed and developing countries is generally based on economic and technological sectors. The term developed countries is used to designate nations that enjoy high per capita income (average income per citizen), high standards of living (the quality and quantity of goods and services available in a society), long life expectancy (the average expected life span of a nation's citizens), and other measurements relating to a high quality of life for the individual. Developed countries are also known as First World countries, industrialized nations, advanced economies, and more economically advanced countries.

2.1.1. Concept of Developed Countries:

Developed countries have industrial growth and enjoy flourishing economy. Developed countries experience marked development and growth in the areas such as transportation, business and education. Developed countries are characterized by a low death rate and low birth rate as well. There is usually a very small gap between the two rates in developed countries. Developed countries are not characterized by shortcomings. They are well-developed in all fronts and are served well by water supplies, amenities, educational institutions, health care concerns. This is because of the fact that people are endowed with awareness about every possible aspect relating to human existence. The absence of shortcomings in the developed countries is possibly due to the fact there is a low birth rate in these countries. Nutrition is available in plenty to mothers and infants in developed countries.

A) Meaning:

A country that has progressed adequately with regard to economic, mortality and demographic indicators, such as Australia and Japan. These countries have access to food, high levels or education and employment and earn high average incomes. Developed countries, also known as industrialized countries or advanced economies, refer to nations that have achieved a high level of economic and social development. These countries typically have well-established infrastructure, advanced industries, a high standard of living, and a strong institutional framework.

B) Definition:

The following is the definition of developed countries.

1) Kofi Annan, former Secretary General of the UN:

"A developed country is one that allows all its citizens to enjoy a free and healthy life in a safe environment."

2) The United Nations Development Programme (UNDP):

The UNDP defines developed countries as "those with a high level of human development, based on indicators such as life expectancy, education, and income per capita. They maintain the Human Development Index (HDI) to measure and compare human development across nations."

3) Professor Adam Szirmai:

"Developed countries are those that have achieved a significant level of industrialization, technological progress, and economic diversification, resulting in sustained high living standards for the majority of their population."

2.1.2. Characteristics of Developed Countries:

Usually, a developed economy automatically makes a country developed. This is often the common notion. But a developed nation is developed in all aspects including health, GDP or Gross Domestic Product, politics, Gross National Product or GNP, etc. Human development Index, per capita income of people, and the standard of living of the citizens are also certain useful factors to take into consideration. When all such aspects are taken care of, and the economy is stably growing, only then can a country be designated as developed. There are certain factors that we have discussed below that mark a developed economy:

1) **Human Development Index:**
   It is a measure introduced by the UN. This particular parameter is used to determine the extent of human development in a nation. HDI is a measure put between 0 to 1- the higher it is- the more developed the economy is. GDI and GNP usually give only the income and productivity of a nation. HDI measures how this income has turned into social development standards like health or education. Other factors that are also considered, such as availability of healthcare facilities, child mortality rate, access to quality education, the average number of years spent in school. HDI can also change according to the ability of the children to implement the knowledge gained in school in real-life situations. All these factors and many more are useful in determining the HDI of a country. HDI is incorporating more in comparison to GDP or GNP. It is citizen-specific and more reliable. Any developed country should have high education, literacy, and health levels.

2) **Per Capita Income:**
   It is the average money that a person receives in a year within a particular region. We calculate it by dividing total income in the given country by the total population that was last estimated. Developed countries always have a high value of per capita income. High per capita income indicates financial security and economic development. It is also indicative of high economic growth and a high standard of living. The Gross Domestic Product is sometimes used as a means to calculate the per capita income. In simple words; GDP is the final cost of the product manufactured in the country. GDP and per capita income are primarily correlated. Per capita income means how much revenue the people within a region are earning. If it is high, it would indicate that people have excellent living standards. Similarly, if the GDP is high, it means that the nation is developed and has stable economic growth. Both are essential factors in determining the extent of growth that a country has experienced in a particular time frame.

3) **Industrialization:**
   Developed countries have high rates of employment and manufacturing. As opposed to emerging economies that depend on agriculture, an improved economy depends

on the industry. The larger the industrial setups, the better are the economic development. Developed economies have modern technology. Not only this, all people within the country have access to excellent facilities and technical advancements. Such countries have high manufacturing rates and more export than imports. The higher export rate will bring in more profits and ensure that the economy is consistently growing. And this consistency will lead to increased industrialization. Hence, levels of manufacturing are a great determiner of a country's development.

4) **Political Stability:**

Political stability is a relatively new measure of a country's development. The World Bank initiated this factor. It acts as a useful parameter in determining the development of a nation. Developed countries are politically stable have low to no corruption, and people have high respect for the country's laws. Good governance is a way of making sure that there is a right amount of transparency in public affairs, along with high employment rates. It makes sure that the level of corruption is low and ensures that the employee is solely based on proper qualification, eligibility, and ranking. Ensuring this will automatically provide a stable and robust government body. The global governance index is measured between -2.5 and +2.15. A positive 2.5 is the highest rating any country may have. Higher the number more developed is the state.

5) **Freedom:**

A developed country provides various forms of freedom to its citizens. These forms of freedom are considered as the fundamental rights of the citizens. Hence, a developed nation respects and abides by these rights. These fundamental rights include the right to worship, settle anywhere within the country, marry, own land or property, and gain access to information regarding the governmental policies, etc. In less developed or developing nations, certain people are deprived of such fundamental rights. There are many restrictions on the people, and they aren't allowed to do certain things out of their own free will. Depriving your people of such freedom can significantly affect the status of a country.

6) **Better Living Standards:**

The people in developed nations have a high standard of living. By rule of thumb, the people living in a developed country have a higher standard of living in comparison to those living in developing nations. The reason is that a more massive chunk of the population has the financial stability to purchase quality goods and services with expensive rates. It includes excellent health care, housing conditions, appropriate sanitation facilities, and access to education. Other than this, there is a spirit of goodwill among people since they face little economic hardships. Excellent living standards indicate that people are employed and earning. It also shows the level of participation of the population in the country's development. There is access to clean water as well as the environment. People prefer using goods produced in one's own country as opposed to exports. This aspect helps to determine how self-sufficient and independent a country is when it comes to sustaining its population.

7) Gross Domestic Product:

This is perhaps the most common measure of an economy's development. As mentioned before, GDP is an essential determiner of a country's rate of development. Unlike HDI, this factor is economy-oriented. Gross domestic product refers to the total value of goods and services produced within a country. Developed countries have a high GDP. However, the gross domestic product doesn't always signify a developed economy. There are countries like Qatar that have high GDP but are still considered to be growing. It is mainly because the major part of the population continues to face economic setbacks.

8) Education:

Developed nations make sure that all its citizens have access to a good education. There are a good number of children enrolling in school each year, and the standard of education is high. There is excellent communication between the school and its students. The premise is well maintained and safe. The average number of years that the students spend in school in a country determines its level of education. The ability to apply the acquired knowledge is the practical life helps to understand the quality of education. In developing nations, a massive number of children are deprived of education. Also, the quality of education provided may include weak or unsatisfactory. These two reasons mainly affect the quality of the upcoming citizenry. This problem does not occur in a developed nation.

9) Knowledge-Economy:

Knowledge economy refers to developing valuable knowledge such as procedures, designs, software, and formulations. It is the increase in creative input by the people. There are scientific and technical breakthroughs marking a good economy. People within a developed economy have a more significant fraction of working in the service sector. This implies more lawyers, doctors, engineers, architects, and so on.

10) Service Economy:

The service economy is a parameter that measures a nation's overall output of services. These services may include travel, restaurants, business services, software made available to the citizens. Developed countries focus on providing more of these services to this public. The reason is that these services will ultimately lead to economic growth. Providing high-quality products and services will lead to an increase in economic output.

11) The Role of the Government:

The government in a developed economy is stable and well-founded. The people are free to choose their leader and are happy with the prevailing societal norms. The role which the government plays has a lot to say about the kind of economy which exists. In a developed economy, the government can maintain law and order. The public infrastructure is good, whereas there is easy access to social facilities like health, education, and transport. The governance is stable, with little fluctuation in the political and social conditions.

12) The Role of the Household:

A household includes the general public, which makes the population. The role of the house is pronounced in a developed economy. People in developed countries contribute significantly to the country's income. The private sector is well established and flourishing. There are industries and a large number of entrepreneurs. If the economy is not very capitalistic, then the service sector makes a large part of the economy.

13) Health:

Efficient healthcare services, the introduction of vaccinations, developed medical facilities, etc. are important factors that affect the overall health of the population. Accesses to modern medical facilities, free healthcare services, low under-5 mortality rates, etc. are the characteristics of a developed nation. Contrary to this, in developing countries, a significant chunk of the population is deprived of free medical facilities. The infant mortality rate may be high, and the total fertility rate may be inconsistent.

14) Total Fertility Rate:

In simple words, total fertility is defined as the average number of offspring born to a woman during her reproductive age. In a hypothetical world where resources are unlimited, this rate can go up to 25-30 children. But in reality, the funds are limited. Hence, a country cannot afford to have a high total fertility rate. Usually, in a developed nation, the fertility rate ranges from one to three children. The concept of a nuclear family is encouraged. On the other hand, in a developing country, the total fertility rate ranges from three to seven. Here, the concept of a more substantial or joint family is predominant. This creates pressure on the resources available. This leads to unequal distribution and degradation of resources.

2.2. Developing Countries:

The total major countries of the world are 182 out of which only 34 are developed and remaining 148 are under developed. Developing Country (DC) is a nation which, compare to developed nations, lacks industrialization, infrastructure, and developed agriculture developed natural resources and suffers from a low per capita income as a result. Developing countries and developed countries are differentiating on the bases of self-esteem, freedom of choice and influence of externals. A country where the average income of the people is much lower than that of developed countries, the economy depends upon a few export crops and where farming is conducted by primary methods is called developing country. Rapid population growth is causing the shortage of food in many developing countries.

2.2.1 Concept of Developing Countries:

Concept of Developing countries explained with following points:

A) Meaning:

Developing countries are those that have a low gross domestic product (GDP) per person. They tend to rely on agriculture as their prime industry. They have not quite reached economic maturity, although there are a number of definitions for this term. This type of country is so often defined by its economic output. There has been a lot of debate as to where to draw the line between a developed country and a developing one, which can be seen by the lack of one single meaning for the term. The United Nations has some rules for distinguishing between developed and developing countries. The World Bank has stopped using these terms in favor of others, such as low-income or lower-middle-income economies, based on gross national income (GNI) per person.

B) Definitions:

The following are the definitions of developing countries:

1) According to United Nations Experts:

"A developing country is that in which per capita income is low when compared to the per capita incomes of U.S.A., Canada, Australia and Western Europe."

2) According to Prof. R. Nurkse:

"Under developed countries are those which when compared with the advanced countries, are under-equipped with capital in relation to their population and natural resources."

3) According to Michal P. Tadaro:

"The under developed country is that which has low levels of living (absolute poverty, poor health, poor education and other social services), low self-esteem (low respect, honour, dignity) and limited freedom (freedom from external influence and dominance, freedom of choice etc.)."

2.2.2 Characteristics of Developing Countries:

Developing countries are also called poor countries. Sometimes they are often called underdeveloped economics. According to the UN criteria, countries with less than $400 level of per capita income countries are designated as low income countries and countries with less than $750 percapita income as called less developed economics. The following are the main characteristics of developing countries:

A) Economic Characteristics:

Following are the economic characteristics of Developing Countries:

1) Low Per Capita Income:

Under developed economy is characterized by low per capital income. India per capital income is very low as compared to the advanced countries. For example the capital income of India was 460 dollar, in 2000. Whereas their capita income of U.S.A in 2000 was 83 times than India. This trend of difference of per capita income between under developed and advanced countries is gradually increasing in present times. India not only the per capita income is low but also the income is unequally distributed. This mal-distribution of income and wealth makes the problem of poverty in ore critical and acute and stands an obstacle in the process of economic progress.

2) Heavy Population Pressure:

The Indian economy is facing the problem of population explosion. It is clearly evident from the total population of India which was 102.67 crores in 2001 census. It is the second highest populated country China being the first. India's population has reached 110 crores. All the under developed countries are characterized by high birth rate which stimulates the growth of population; the fast rate of growth of population necessitates a higher rate of economic growth to maintain the same standard of living. The failure to sustain the living standard makes the poor and under developed countries poor and under developed.

3) Pre-dominance of Agriculture:

Occupational distribution of population in India clearly reflects the backwardness of the economy. One of the basis characteristics of an under developed economy is that agriculture contributes a very large portion in the national income and a very high proportion of working population is engaged in agriculture.

4) Unemployment:

There is larger unemployed and under employment is another important feature of Indian economy. In under developed countries labor is an abundant factor. It is not possible to provide gainful employment the entire population. Lack of job opportunities disguised unemployed is created' in the agriculture fields. There deficiency of capital formation.

5) Low Rate of Capital Formation:

In backward economics like India, the rate of capital formation is also low. capital formation mainly depends on the ability and willingness of the people save since the per capita income is low and there is mal-distribution of income and wealth the ability of the people to save is very low in under developed countries for which capital formation is very low.

6) Poor Technology:

The lever of technology is a common factor in under developed economy. India economy also suffers from this typical feature of technological backwardness. The techniques applied in agriculture industries milling and other economic fields are primitive in nature.

7) Backward Institutional and Social Frame Work:

The social and institutional frame work in under developed countries like India is hopelessly backward which is a strong obstacle to any change in the form of production. Moreover religious institutions such as caste system, joint family universal marriage affects the economic life of the people.

8) Underutilization of Resources:

India is a poor land. So our people remain economically backwards for the lack of utilization of resources of the country.

9) Price Instability:

Price instability is also a basis feature of Indian economy. In almost all the underdeveloped countries like India there is continuous price instability. Shortage of essential commodities and gap between consumption aid productions increase the price persistently. Rising trend of price creates a problem to maintain standard of living of the common people.

10) High Dependence on Agriculture

Agriculture is the main occupation in developing countries. More than 70 percent of active labor force is engaged in this primary sector. Population increases and the increased labor stick to agriculture thereby over burdening the firm size. There is low output per head.

11) Lack of Basic Infrastructures

The factors that help for development are called infrastructures. Good road system, highways, telephone, services, big dams and canals, banks and financial services are some examples of the necessary infrastructures.

12) General Poverty

Developing countries are poor. By definition, GDP and Per Capita Income are at low level. General living standard of people in these countries is very slow. Poverty is visibly disturbing every aspect of life. General health services for people are insignificant. The life expectancy at birth does not exceed 60 years.

B) Demographic Characteristics:

Developing countries are characterized by a range of demographic features that reflect their stage of development and socio-economic conditions. While there can be variations among developing countries, the following demographic characteristics are often observed:

1) Backward Population Explosion:

Another common feature of lower developing nations is population pressure due to high growth rate and reduction in death rate. Basic needs like food, clothing, housing, education, sanitations and health facilities are not available for the huge portion of population in these countries.

2) Brain Drain:

An outflow of the best, brightest and talented student from poor nations to rich nations is called brain drain. There is less reward for the talent, which causes an outflow of best brain in the backward countries. Reward is not paid in accordance with the capability, skill and efficiency in less developed countries.

3) High Population Growth:

Developing countries tend to have higher population growth rates compared to developed countries. Factors such as high birth rates, limited access to family planning, cultural norms, and inadequate healthcare contribute to population growth.

4) Youthful Population:

Developing countries typically have a larger proportion of young people, often referred to as a "youth bulge." This can present both opportunities and challenges for these countries in terms of education, employment, and social development.

5) High Fertility Rates:

Fertility rates, which measure the average number of children born per woman, are generally higher in developing countries. Cultural, social, and economic factors, as well as limited access to contraception and family planning services, contribute to higher fertility rates.

6) Lower Life Expectancy:

Developing countries tend to have lower life expectancy compared to developed countries. Factors such as inadequate healthcare infrastructure, limited access to quality healthcare services, poverty, malnutrition, and higher prevalence of diseases contribute to lower life expectancy.

7) Rural-urban Migration:

Developing countries often experience significant rural-urban migration as people move from rural areas to cities in search of better economic opportunities and improved living conditions. This can lead to rapid urbanization and the growth of informal settlements.

8) Higher Dependency Ratios:

Developing countries frequently have higher dependency ratios, which measure the proportion of the non-working population (children and elderly) to the working-age population. This places a burden on the working-age population to support dependents, impacting economic development and social welfare systems.

9) Limited access to Education:

Developing countries may face challenges in providing universal access to quality education. Issues such as lack of infrastructure, insufficient funding, cultural barriers, and gender disparities can limit educational opportunities, particularly for marginalized populations.

C) Technological Characteristics:

Developing countries often exhibit specific technological characteristics that reflect their current stage of development, level of technological infrastructure, and access to technology. While there can be variations among developing countries, the following technological characteristics are commonly observed:

1) Limited technological infrastructure:

Developing countries may have inadequate technological infrastructure, including telecommunications networks, internet connectivity, transportation systems, and energy grids. This can hamper the widespread adoption and utilization of advanced technologies.

2) Digital Divide:

Developing countries often face a digital divide, where there is an unequal distribution of access to information and communication technologies (ICTs) between urban and rural areas, as well as across socioeconomic groups. This divide can hinder economic development and limit participation in the digital economy.

3) Adoption of Mobile Technology:

Mobile technology has become a significant driver of technological advancement in developing countries. Due to the relatively low cost and widespread availability of mobile phones, these devices are often the primary means of accessing the internet and digital services in these regions.

4) Leapfrogging:

In some cases, developing countries have the opportunity to leapfrog traditional stages of technological development. They can bypass older technologies and directly adopt more advanced solutions. For example, some developing countries have seen widespread adoption of mobile payment systems without relying heavily on traditional banking infrastructure.

5) Technology Transfer and Adaptation:

Developing countries often rely on technology transfer from developed countries. This involves acquiring technologies, knowledge, and expertise from external sources and adapting them to local conditions. This enables developing countries to leverage existing innovations rather than reinventing the wheel.

6) Emphasis on Appropriate Technology:

Developing countries often focus on appropriate technology solutions that are affordable, adaptable, and suitable for local contexts. These technologies are often designed to address specific needs, such as access to clean water, renewable energy, healthcare, and agriculture.

7) Growing Tech Startup Ecosystems:

Many developing countries are witnessing the emergence of vibrant tech startup ecosystems. These ecosystems foster innovation, entrepreneurship, and technological advancements by providing support structures, access to funding, and networking opportunities for local startups.

D) Socio-Cultural Characteristics:

Following are the Socio-Cultural characteristics of Developing Countries:

1) High Degree of Illiteracy:

Illiteracy rate is very high in developing countries while it is almost zero in rich countries. There is lack of technical education and training centers, which is necessary for economic growth and development.

2) Low Level of Organisation:

There is absence of developed minded leadership in economic activities in third world nations. Decision making power of entrepreneur is very low due to illiteracy, less training and backward techniques. Most of educational institutions are producing employees rather than employers.

3) Low Self-esteem:

There is less respect, honour and dignity of people in the lower developed countries. People are honoured due to their powers, relations and castes instead of capabilities. There is poverty, poor health, poor education and shortage of other social services. Government and population of poor countries are under the external influence.

4) Un-productive Expenditures:

Population mostly copies the styles of population of developed nations due to demonstration action in developing economies. Their consumption activities not only move around their income but also depend upon the relatives, friends and locality. They spend more on birth, death, marriages and various other ceremonies etc. which reduces their savings and investment.

5) Political Instability:

There is political instability in the most of the developing countries. There are a lot of clashes between government and the opposition that is a cause to reduction in domestic as well as foreign investment. Political instability keeps low the level of economic development.

6) Influence of Feudal Lords:

The poor class is under the influence of feudal lords and tribal heads in lower developed nations. The feudal lords want to keep the people backward and do not appreciate the development of the poor.

7) Govt. Control by Wealthy Persons:

Wealthy persons, landlords and elite class not only control the government but also they have full control over all the major sectors of the economy in poor countries. This rich class is not interested to solve the problems of the poor for their welfare but they make government policies for their own improvement.

8) Frequent Changes in Fiscal Policy:

Revenues and expenditures policy of government is not stable in developing countries. Government has to change the fiscal policy according to the will of its own people. Industrialists are the main controller of the government and they adjust the fiscal policy in accordance with their own benefits.

E) Political Characteristics:

Developing countries often exhibit certain political characteristics that reflect their stage of development, governance structures, and political dynamics. While there can be variations among developing countries, the following political characteristics are commonly observed:

1) Political Instability:

Developing countries may experience higher levels of political instability compared to developed countries. Factors such as weak institutions, ethnic or religious tensions, corruption, economic disparities, and governance challenges can contribute to political volatility, including frequent changes in government, political unrest, and social upheavals.

2) Democratic Transitions:

Many developing countries have undergone or are in the process of transitioning from autocratic or authoritarian regimes to more democratic systems. This often involves struggles for political freedoms, the establishment of democratic institutions, the protection of human rights, and the fostering of civic participation.

3) Governance Challenges:

Developing countries often face governance challenges, including corruption, lack of transparency, inefficiency, and a weak rule of law. These issues can hinder economic development, erode public trust, and impede effective decision-making and service delivery.

4) Economic Policy-making:

Developing countries frequently grapple with formulating and implementing effective economic policies. Balancing economic development, poverty reduction, income distribution, and attracting investment while maintaining social stability is often a complex challenge.

5) Developmental State Approach:

Some developing countries adopt a developmental state approach, where the government plays a proactive role in guiding economic development and industrialization. This involves interventions such as strategic planning, industrial policies, investment in infrastructure, and targeted support for key sectors.

6) Dependency on Foreign Aid:

Many developing countries rely on foreign aid and assistance from international organizations to support their development efforts. This dependency can shape political dynamics, influence policy decisions, and introduce external influences in domestic affairs.

7) Ethnic and Cultural Diversity:

Developing countries often have diverse populations with multiple ethnic, linguistic, and cultural groups. Managing and accommodating this diversity can be a significant political challenge, requiring inclusive governance, power-sharing arrangements, and respect for minority rights.

8) Regional and Global Power Dynamics:

Developing countries often navigate complex regional and global power dynamics. They may engage in alliances, negotiations, and partnerships to secure resources, market access, development assistance, and address geopolitical pressures.

F) Other Characteristics:

The following are the other characteristics of developing countries:

1) Lack of Development of Infrastructure:

In underdeveloped countries there will be lack of development of infrastructure. In such countries facilities of transportation and communication will not be expanded adequately. One a small fraction of the population of such countries will have access to hydro-electricity power. Expansion of banking and financial institutions will be inadequate. For this reason the farmers of the rural areas will have to depend upon high interest rates of landlords and money lenders. The farmers are even exploited by the people of such class. People have to travel on foot for weeks to go from one place to another. So, lack of development of infrastructures is also the major problem of the underdeveloped countries.

2) Gender Discrimination:

In underdeveloped countries gender discrimination will be in intensive form. In such countries role of women will be negligible. There will be majority of males in every sector of employment. As a result women will be limited to only household works. Women don't have right in acquiring parental wealth and property. Literacy of females is also very low as compared to that of males. In rural areas females are even deprived from getting enough food. Thus in underdeveloped countries there will be a great discrimination between males and females.

3) Low Utilization of Natural Resources:

In underdeveloped countries natural resources are used partially or in very small quantity. In such countries the true facts about the availability of natural resources will not be known. The utilization of the available natural resources will also be very low. In such countries the various natural resources such as forest resources, water resources, minerals, etc. will be available in large quantity. But these natural resources will not be utilized properly for the long-run economic development. Despite the availability of natural resources in large quantity such countries will not be able to exploit those resources for the benefit of the country. For example, Nepal has the capacity of producing 83,000 megawatts of hydro-electricity, but the production of hydro-electricity is very low. Not even one percent has been produced.

4) Lack of Entrepreneurs:

In underdeveloped countries due to various reasons there will be lack of entrepreneurs. Lack of capital, lack of technical knowledge, very limited markets etc. are the main reasons for the lack of entrepreneurs in underdeveloped countries. Due to these various reasons the businessmen are not interested in investing in such countries. In such countries due to excessive poverty also there will very few investors or entrepreneurs. In such countries there will also be lack of policies which motivate investment. In such countries there will be few industrialists only and they will exploit consumers by creating monopoly over various goods and services. This is because the main objective of such entrepreneurs is profit earning rather the economic development of the country.

5) Unemployment Problem:

Unemployment problem is another main characteristic of underdeveloped countries. In such countries due to lack of trained human resources major fraction of the population remains unemployed. Therefore in such countries there will be problems like unemployment, semi-unemployment and seasonal unemployment. The main cause of unemployment is the lack of alternative employment opportunities in other sectors besides agriculture. Semi-unemployment and seasonal unemployment arises in agricultural sector. This is because in underdeveloped countries farmers remain unemployed for rest of the year after working for 3 or 4 months. Likewise in underdeveloped countries agriculture also depends upon season. Therefore if rainfall is on time and sufficient then farmers will have employment for some time only. But if effect of climate is adverse then farmers will be unemployed for even longer time. In underdeveloped countries there will be lack of alternative employment opportunities. Therefore large fraction of population will be unemployed.

❖❖❖❖❖❖❖❖

Review Questions

Q. 1. Answer in 100 Words:

1) State the Concept of Developed Countries.
2) Explain the Concept of Developing Countries.
3) State the Demographic Characteristics of Developing Countries.
4) Explain the Technological Characteristics of Developing Countries.
5) Discuss the Political Characteristics of Developing Countries

Q. 2. Answer in 200 Words:

1) Explain the Characteristics of Developed Countries.
2) Discuss the Economic Characteristics of Developing Countries.
3) Explain the Socio-Cultural Characteristics of Developing Countries.

Q. 3. Answer in 400 Words:

1) What is Developed Countries? Explain the Characteristics of Developed Countries.
2) What is Developing Countries? State the Characteristics of Developing Countries.

Q.4 Write Short Note on Following:

1) Demographic Characteristics.
2) Technological Characteristics.
3) Economic Characteristics.
4) Political Characteristics.
5) Socio-Cultural Characteristics.

❖❖❖❖❖❖❖❖

UNIT 3

Constraints to Development Process

Introduction:

The process of economic development is an important instance of the inter animation of policy, contingency, and justice. Governments construct development strategies based on a variety of political and social objectives; this process may be characterised in terms of a decision-making process based on instrumental rationality. The outcomes of these strategies depend heavily on a variety of factors, only some of which are within the control of policy maker's world commodity markets, the behavior of powerful outsiders, weather and climate variability, and so forth. And the outcomes and implementations of development strategies unavoidably raise problems of justice. This is so because they have deeply significant distributive effects that may endure over many generations. Obstacles in the way of economic development, and hamper economic progress. These features emerge out of economic, social, political, religious and institutional factors.

3.1. Vicious Circle of Poverty:

The cycle of poverty is a phenomenon where poor families become impoverished for at least three generations, i.e. for enough time that the family includes no surviving ancestors who possess and can transmit the intellectual, social, and cultural capital necessary to stay out of or change their impoverished condition. In calculations of expected generation length and ancestor lifespan, the lower median age of parents in these families is offset by the shorter lifespan in many of these groups.

A) Meaning:

Vicious circle of poverty means that poverty begets poverty. In other words poverty is the cause and effect of poverty. Vicious circle of poverty is such a circular activity whose beginning is poverty and whose end is also poverty. It is like a patient who is a patient because of his physical weakness and who is physically weak because he is a patient.

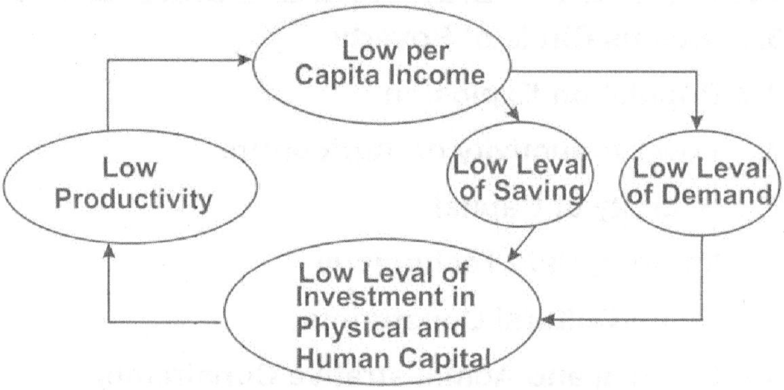

Fig. 3.1: Vicious Circle of Poverty

B) Definitions:

The following are definitions of Vicious Circle of Poverty

1) Nurkse.

"Vicious Circle of Poverty implies circular constellation of forces tending to act and react upon one another in such a way as to keep a poor country in a state poverty."

2) Walter Krause:

"The term vicious circle as it applies to the environment in countries refers to an interrelationship of cause and effect that operates so as to keep the economy in its own shortcomings."

3.1.1. Causes of Vicious Circle of Poverty:

The following are the causes of vicious circle of poverty:

1) Supply Side of Vicious Circle:

Supply side of vicious circle indicates that in underdeveloped countries, productivity is so low that it is not enough for capital formation. According to Samuelson, "The backward nations cannot get their heads above water because their production is so low that they can spare nothing for capital formation by which their standard of living could be raised." In the words of Prof. Nurkse on the supply side there is small capacity to save resulting from low level of national income. The low real income is a reflection of low productivity, which in turn is due largely to the lack of capital. The lack of capital is a result of the small capacity to save and so the circle is complete.

Low Income → Low Saving → Low Investment → Low Production → Low Income

The supply side of vicious circle can be illustrated with the help of a fig .3.2

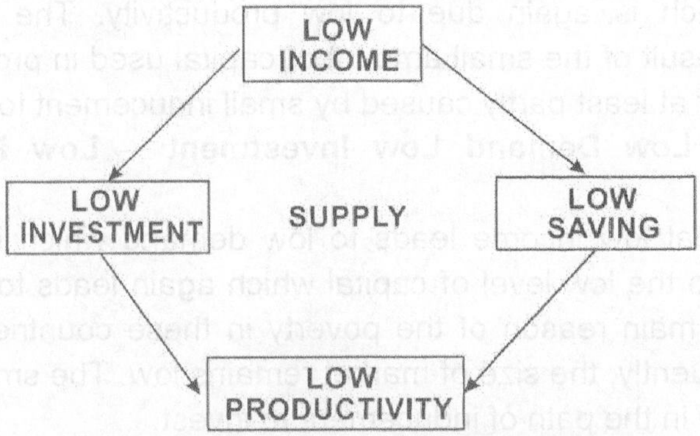

Fig. 3.2: Supply Side of Vicious Circle

Reflects the UDCs are poor. In these countries poverty refers to low real income. Real income remains low due to low level of capital and capital is low because of low level of saving. The reason of low saving is low level of income. Those, it becomes clear from the above analysis, that the main reason of low level of poverty and income is the low level of saving. Consequently, investment is not possible in production channels. A man can save only when his real income exceeds consumption. Generally, in UDC, society is divided into two groups' viz.; rich and poor.

In such countries, majority of farmers are from poor groups. Their income is very low because they are engaged in subsistence farming. The methods of cultivation are old and unskilled. The productivity of labour is low due to unskilled labour, disguised unemployment and immobility of labour. Under such situation, a huge chunck of national product is consumed on consumption purposes. In this way, they lack in saving, investment and so the capital formation. Although, the rich group of the society is in a position to save. But, they spend their saving on luxurious goods instead of saving. They gave preference to foreign products. Thus, their demand does not enlarge the size of the market. Basically, in an economy, investment does not depend only on saving, but also on ability to invest and willingness to invest. These countries lacks in investment facilities due to low level of demand. The quantity of investment depends on able entrepreneurs. Able entrepreneurs have to take risk and put hard work to set up a new industry. The social atmosphere of the rich class is such that they do not dare to take risk. They prefer to put some labourers on work. Moreover, in UDCs, there exist medium income group who prefer to work in trade, services etc. instead of capital formation. The main reasons responsible for this are lack of capital for investment in industries, lack of industrial finance, lack of skilled labour, lack of transportation and social overhead etc.

2) Demand Side of Vicious Circle:

According to Prof. Nurkse, "On the demand side, the inducement of invest may he low because of the small purchasing power of the people, which is due to the small real income, which is again due to low productivity. The level of productivity however, is the result of the small amount of capital used in production which in turn may be caused or at least partly caused by small inducement to invest.

Low Income → Low Demand Low Investment → Low Productivity → Low Income

Fig. 3.3 shows that low income leads to low demand which in turn results in low investment and so the low level of capital which again leads to low productivity and low income. The main reason of the poverty in these countries is the low level of demand. Consequently, the size of market remains low. The small size of the market becomes a hurdle in the path of inducement to invest.

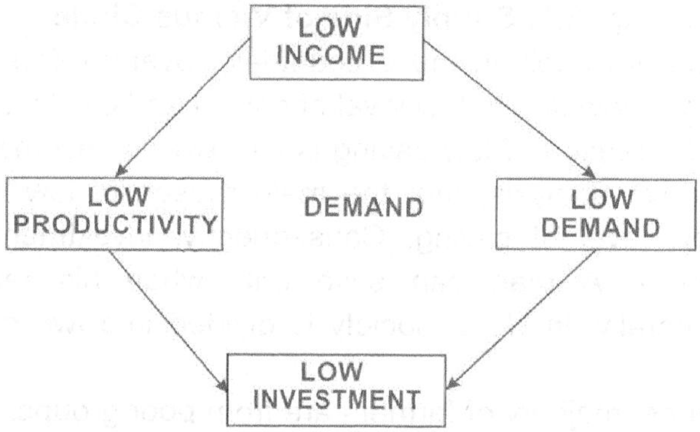

Fig. 3.3: Demand Side of Vicious Circle

Thus, the investors do not establish industries on large scale and productivity remains low and so the income. In order to prove this, Prof. Nurkse has cited many examples. For instance, an entrepreneur will not establish a modern shoe factory in a country where the people are poverty ridden and unable to purchase shoes. Similarly, iron and steel industry in Chile will produce so much iron and steel in three hours that the entire demand of the country can be fulfilled. Thus, according to Nurkse, "In underdeveloped countries, on demand side, low purchasing power of the people results in low productivity."

3) Vicious Circle of Market Imperfections:

Meier and Baldwin have described a third vicious circle based on capital deficiency due to market imperfections. In underdeveloped countries, resources are underdeveloped and people are economically backward. Existence of market imperfections prevents optimum allocation and utilization of natural resources and the result is underdevelopment and this, in turn, leads to economic backwardness. The development of natural resources depends upon the character of human resources. But due to lack of skill and low level of knowledge, natural resources will remain unutilized, under-utilized and misutilised. In the words of Meier and Baldwin, "Underdeveloped resources are, therefore, both a consequence and cause of the backward people. The more economically backward are the people, the less developed will be natural resources, lesser the development of natural resources more the people are economically backward." The vicious circle caused by Market Imperfections is shown as under.

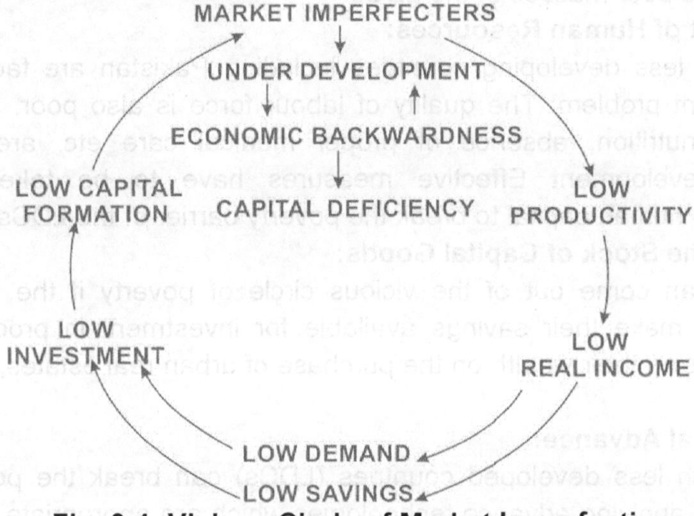

Fig. 3.4: Vicious Circle of Market Imperfections:

The vicious circle of poverty is a result of the various vicious circles which were on the sides of supply of and demand for capital. As a result capital formation remains low productivity and low real incomes. Thus, the country is caught in vicious circles of poverty which are mutually aggravating and it is very difficult to break them.

3.1.2. Measures of Vicious Circle of Poverty:

Remaining poor is certainly no crime. The accepting of poverty and allowing it to continue is certainly a crime. Briefly, the vicious circle of poverty can be broken in developing countries by adopting following measures.

1) Increase in Savings:

The vicious of circle of poverty can be broken by making serious efforts in increasing the volume of real savings both at the level of in development the govt. The govt. can also mobilize foreign savings for capital formation country.

2) Higher Per Capital Growth Rate:

The per capital growth rate should be higher than the rate of growth of population. This objective is achieved by increasing the level of employment in the country and reducing the rate of population growth. If the rate of increase in real per capital income is the same as the rate of growth of population, the real income per person will remain unchanged.

3) Efficient Use of Natural Resources:

The less developed countries (LDC) are not making the efficient use of the natural resources available to them. At present the multinational companies (MNCs) of the advanced countries are exploiting these resources more for their own economic benefits. The economic advantages of the natural resources must pass on to the benefits of the poor masses of the LDCs.

4) Employment of Human Resources:

Many of the less developing countries including Pakistan are faced with serious unemployment problem. The quality of labour force is also poor. The low level of literacy, malnutrition, absence of proper medical care etc. are all barriers to economic development Effective measures have to be taken for sufficient investment in human capital to break the poverty barrier of the LDCs.

5) Increasing the Stock of Capital Goods:

The LDCs can come out of the vicious circle of poverty if the wealthy class is motivated to make their savings available for investment in productive activates rather than using their wealth on the purchase of urban real estates, precious metals etc.

6) Technological Advance:

The people in less developed countries (LDCs) can break the poverty barrier by adopting and applying advance technologies which are appropriate to the resources available to them.

7) Role of the Advanced Nations:

The advanced nations can helps the less developed countries in breaking the poverty barrier by:

a) Expanding volume of trade with them.

b) Increasing the flow of private and public capital in basic infrastructure.

c) Provision of direct aid in basic social sectors such as education, health etc.

d) Provision of soft loans for development.

e) Writing off loans.

8) Role for the Government:

The government in the less developed country is in the key position to deal effectively with social institutional obstacles to growth and breaking out the vicious circle of poverty. It can greatly root out political corruption and bribery. It can provide incentives to save and invest. It can increase agricultural production by introducing effective land reforms in the country.

3.2. Population Explosion:

Population explosion is the rapid increase of a population. Most developing countries have contributed to the drastic population increase over the past hundred years. India and the other developing countries are facing the problem of population explosion.

These countries fail to control the growth of population due to poverty and illiteracy. In the same way, in many countries, the economic development rate is lower than the rate of population growth. So if there is economic development in these countries then it cannot be seen because of the huge population growth. This economic development rate is failed to fulfill various needs of the growing population. In other words, population growth rate has become an obstacle in the economic development of these countries. To improve the economic development and poverty of these countries, they have to control the growth of population.

3.2.1 Meaning of Population Explosion:

The term, 'population explosion' refers to the sudden and dramatic increase in the number of human beings. Population explosion means tremendous growth in the population of a particular region which results in the shortfall of facilities and increase in the poverty and unemployment. According to Malthusian, population is an uncontrolled problem in the underdeveloped countries and its reason is rising up of progeny capacity of human being, According to some economists, population explosion is the second state of population transition. Its main cause is no decrease in the death rate due to economic development. But there are no decreases in the birth rate. According to some economist there are three stages of population.

3.2.2 Stages of Population Explosion:

Frank Notestein has used the concept/term Population transaction for the first time. According to population Transition theory, there are three Stages of population growth:

1) **Pre-transition or Primary Stage:**
   In this stage, both the birth and death rates are high. It is due to the lack of family planning facilities, misunderstanding, lack of sufficient health services, infant, death rate, the way of thinking of people. In the same way, death rate is high because of under-nutrition. Poverty, superstitious beliefs and illiteracy are the g characteristics of such population. In this stage, there is neither growth in the population nor the problems of increased population.
2) **Transition or Population Growth Stage:**
   In this stage, there is decrease in death rate but birth rate is not decrease in that proportion. Population increases rapidly. The standard of living is high facilities such as education, health, medical facilities are developed. So decrease in death rate. But the birth rate is not decreased. So increases rapidly and, hence, large number of population is living under the line of poverty. This population situation is called as population explosion. The population in India since last decade is an example of such population explosion.

3) **After-transition or Population Debilitation Stage:**
The birth rate is decreased in this stage. There is development in family planning facilities. There is increase in industrialization, urbanization and education. It results in the decrease of population growth. Due to urbanization, people have to think about a small family. There is development in employment due to industrialization. Importance to female education is given and this is the way to happy life. To maintain high standard of living, people try to keep their family limited. It results in small family. So the population growth becomes low and population problems are lessened. It helps in stabilization of population.

3.2.3 Problems Due to Over Population Explosion:

Following are the problems which create due to over population explosion.

1) **Man and Land Ratio:**
With the excessive growth of population, the load of population goes on increasing on the available land. Especially, when the land is limited and population which depends upon such land is excessive, the land is used for more production again and again, Crops are taken continuously. Due to the repeated use it causes soil pollution and productivity of land is lowered down. To increase productivity, chemical fertilizer are used which resultantly causes soil pollution.

2) **Deforestation:**
Due to the growth of population, forests are chopped down for making the land for inhabitation and for farming purpose, in the same Way; there is continuous need for wood and other things which result in deforestation. Due to the unemployment, people chopped down the trees; kill the animals for their homes skin, hair and other parts of their body. Because of the deforestation on a large scale, the equilibrium of environment is not maintained. The/ ratio / proportion of carbon dioxide increases in the air. It results in global warming. It has ill-effects on the biodiversity. Due to the deforestation, the rainfall comes down. There is soil erosion on a large scale. There is possibility of destruction of animal species and rare plant species. ;

3) **Loss of Underground Water Sources:**
With the growth of population, the need for water increases. Water is needed in new settlements and industries on a large scale. The water from lake, river, and dams is used excessively. The underground sources of water start decreasing, as the level of water comes down the animal's species in the water are destructed. The forests on the coasts of rivers and lakes are degraded. The rainfall is short and we have to face the problem of draughts.

4) **Excessive Use of Mineral Resources:**
Many types of minerals are declining due to the excessive use by human being. After some years, the energy resources such as mineral oils may or is likely to

come to an end. With the growth of population the need for mineral oils goes on increasing. Fuel for vehicles is used on a large scale every day. It becomes that alter some years, the mineral oil resources may come to an end. In the same way, the use of these minerals in the vehicle and industrial process many poisonous gases are getting mixed in the air which causes air population Land is dug for getting more and more minerals. It endangers the bask land ecosystems in the region. The balance between various factors is distributed the digging process pollutes the air on large scale whereas the machinery and fuel for running this machinery cause noise and air pollution.

5) Decrease in Per Capita Income:

Due to the over population, there is decrease in per capita income. It results in the poverty malnutrition and the diseases created by it.

6) Urban Problems:

A Dun to over population, the civilization and urbanization speed is high. As the income sources in rural areas are not adequate, people migrate to the cities It result in unplanned a large scale development of cities in the countries like India.

3.2.4 Suggestions for Population Explosion:

Addressing population explosion is a complex and multifaceted issue that requires a comprehensive approach. While there is no one-size-fits-all solution, here are some suggestions that can help address population growth:

1) Access to Family Planning:

Ensuring universal access to affordable and comprehensive family planning services is crucial. This includes education about contraception methods, availability of contraceptives, and reproductive health services. Empowering individuals, particularly women, with the ability to make informed decisions about family size and spacing can help curb population growth.

2) Education and Empowerment of Women:

Promoting gender equality and providing quality education to women and girls can have a significant impact on population growth. Educated women tend to have fewer children, better family planning awareness, and increased opportunities for economic empowerment.

3) Improving Healthcare and Child Survival:

Enhancing healthcare infrastructure and services, particularly in developing countries, can reduce infant and child mortality rates. When parents have confidence that their children will survive into adulthood, they are more likely to have smaller families.

4) Poverty Alleviation and Economic Development:

Addressing poverty and promoting sustainable economic development are crucial to population control. Poverty often contributes to high fertility rates, as larger families can be seen as a means of economic security. By improving living conditions and providing economic opportunities, the motivation for large families can decrease.

5) **Awareness and Education:**
Implementing comprehensive awareness campaigns on the benefits of smaller family sizes, family planning, and reproductive health can help change societal norms and attitudes towards population growth. This includes disseminating information through mass media, community engagement, and educational programs.

6) **Sustainable Development and Environmental Conservation:**
Promoting sustainable development practices, including responsible resource management, renewable energy adoption, and environmental conservation, can help mitigate the strain on resources caused by population growth.

7) **Policy and Governance:**
Governments should prioritize population issues in their policy agendas, implementing effective population policies and programs. This includes integrating population dynamics into national development plans, enacting supportive legislation, and allocating resources to implement and monitor population-related initiatives.

8) **International Cooperation:**
Collaborative efforts among governments, international organizations, and civil society are essential in addressing population growth. Sharing best practices, exchanging knowledge, and providing financial and technical support to developing countries can contribute to sustainable population management.

3.3. Low Productivity of Agriculture:

Agricultural productivity is measured as the ratio of agricultural outputs to agricultural inputs. While individual products are usually measured by weight, their varying densities make measuring overall agricultural output difficult. Therefore, output is usually measured as the market value of final output, which excludes intermediate products such as corn feed used in the meat industry. This output value may be compared to many different types of inputs such as labour and land (yield). These are called partial measures of productivity. Agricultural productivity may also be measured by what is termed total factor productivity (TFP). This method of calculating agricultural productivity compares an index of agricultural inputs to an index of outputs. This measure of agricultural productivity was established to remedy the shortcomings of the partial measures of productivity; notably, it is often hard to identify the factors that cause them to change. Changes in TFP are usually attributed to technological improvements.

3.3.1 Causes of Low Productivity:

The main causes for low productivity of agriculture are broadly of three types:

A) Human Factors:

Human favors are those which are related to training and efficiency of the farmers.

1) Social Atmosphere:

Social climate includes customs and traditions. Indian farmers are illiterate and have no knowledge of the latest techniques of production. He believes in God and is a fatalist in thought. He wastes money on customs and traditions so the social climate is not suitable for agriculture.

2) Pressure of Population on land:

Heavy pressure of population is the main cause of low productivity of Indian agriculture. In 1901, 16.30 core people were dependent on agriculture. The number has gone up to 58.80 cores so per capita cultivable land has reduced from 0.43 hectare to 0.23 hectare. Heavy pressure has led to subdivision and fragmentation of land holdings.

B) Technical Factors:

Technical Factors include techniques and methods of production:

1) Traditional methods of Cultivation:

Traditional methods of cultivation like manual ploughing, two crop patterns and old systems of irrigation are mainly responsible for low productivity of agriculture.

2) Old Implements:

Traditional equipment like wooden ploughs, sickles and spades are commonly used. Tractors & Combines are not so common in use. Due to the use of these old implements agriculture is backward.

3) Insufficient irrigation Facilities:

Indian agriculture is mainly dependent on rain. Even after 60 years of Independence only 40% of the agricultural land has permanent irrigation facilities. Due to improper irrigation facilities, farmers can produce one crop only in a year.

4) Problems of Soil:

Indian soil has many problems like soil erosion, water logging, nitrogen deficiency and swamps. These are the reasons for low productivity of agriculture.

5) Problems of Pests and Diseases of Crops:

Plant diseases like rust and smut and rats, insects and pests destroy large portions of crops.

6) Feeble Cattle:

Due to limited mechanization of Indian agriculture, cattle have a significant place in agriculture. Cattle are generally weak. Farmers have to spend a lot on these cattle. Cattle farming is more time consuming and expensive than tractor farming. So these also increase the cost of agriculture.

7) Lack of Credit Facility:

Credit facilities are inadequate in rural areas. Farmers may not be able to raise credit from rural banks easily. They have to depend on 'Mahajans' and 'Shahukars'.

These money lenders charge a heavy rate of interest. Farmers have to sell their produce at low prices to these money lenders. So farmers have low Income and thus low productivity.

8) Lack of High Yielding Variety (HYV) Seeds:

HYV seeds are not commonly used. Farmers do not understand their significance. They cannot afford to buy them and also these seeds are not easily available.

9) Improper Marketing:

Improper marketing is a significant factor for low productivity of agriculture. Farmers fail to get a suitable price for their produce. Inadequate means of transport forces the farmers to sell their produce to local money lenders at low prices. Due to lack of warehousing facilities, farmers are not able to store their produce when prices are low. So these contribute a lot to low productivity of agriculture.

C) Institutional Factors:

Institutional factors include land holdings and the land system.

1) Small Size of Farms:

Land holdings in India are of very small size. Average size of holding is 2.3 hectare and 70% of the holdings are even less than 2 hectares. Due to these small holdings, mechanized cultivation is difficult. Implements and irrigation facilities are not properly utilized. It affects Indian agriculture.

2) Defective Land Tenure System:

Zamindari system has been an important factor responsible for the low productivity of Indian agriculture. In this system cultivator is not owner of land. Land Lord is the owner of land and he can evict the tenant any time. So the cultivator does not take interest in the development of land and Landlord does not take interest in the development of cultivation. Though Zamindari system was abolished after independence yet the position of cultivator has not improved.

3.3.2 Problems of Low Productivity:

The low productivity of agriculture can present several challenges that hinder the sector's growth and contribute to food insecurity and rural poverty. Some common problems associated with low agricultural productivity include:

1) Limited Access to Technology and Innovation:

Farmers in many regions lack access to modern agricultural technologies, machinery, and innovation. Insufficient investment in research and development, inadequate dissemination of agricultural knowledge, and limited access to improved seeds, fertilizers, and irrigation systems restrict productivity gains.

2) Poor Infrastructure:

Inadequate rural infrastructure, such as roads, irrigation networks, and storage facilities, hampers agricultural productivity. Limited access to markets for selling agricultural products, difficulties in transporting inputs, and post-harvest losses due to inadequate storage facilities contribute to low productivity.

3) **Lack of Mechanization:**

The reliance on manual labor and outdated farming practices limits productivity in agriculture. Insufficient availability and affordability of farm machinery, equipment, and tools impede efficient cultivation, harvesting, and post-harvest activities.

4) **Soil Degradation and Land Fragmentation:**

Soil erosion, nutrient depletion, and land fragmentation reduce agricultural productivity. Unsustainable land use practices, such as improper irrigation and excessive use of chemical inputs, lead to soil degradation, declining fertility, and decreased crop yields.

5) **Lack of Access to Credit and Financial Services:**

Limited access to credit and financial services for small-scale farmers restricts their ability to invest in modern farming techniques, purchase inputs, and adopt new technologies. This financial constraint inhibits productivity-enhancing activities and limits the adoption of improved practices.

6) **Climate Change and Environmental Challenges:**

Climate change-related impacts, such as erratic weather patterns, droughts, floods, and pests, pose significant challenges to agricultural productivity. Farmers may struggle to adapt to changing conditions and face increased risks of crop failures and reduced yields.

7) **Inadequate Agricultural Extension Services:**

Insufficient availability of extension services and limited farmer training and education restrict the dissemination of best agricultural practices. This lack of support hinders farmers' ability to adopt improved techniques, utilize resources efficiently, and enhance productivity.

8) **Lack of Market Integration and Value Addition:**

Limited access to markets and value addition opportunities prevents farmers from obtaining fair prices for their produce. Inefficient marketing systems, lack of market information, and inadequate processing and storage facilities contribute to post-harvest losses and reduced profitability.

3.3.3 Measures of Low Productivity:

Important measures to increase productivity are as follows:

1) **Implementation of Land Reforms:**

Special attempts will have to be made by the State Governments to implement the land reforms legislation forcefully so that the slogan 'land to the tiller' is translated into practice. Unless this is done, the tiller will have no incentive to invest in land and adopt new agricultural techniques. Therefore, land reforms are the first and foremost necessity.

2) Integrated Management of Land and Water Resources:

The total geographical area of the country is 328.7 million hectares, of which only 264.0 million hectares possess potential for biotic production. Of this, 'wastelands' account for 79.5 million hectares leaving only 184.5 million hectares. However, even this area cannot be regarded as being in good health. This proves the urgency for an integrated and efficient management policy directed towards better utilisation of our land and water resources.

3) Improved Seeds:

Improved seeds can play an important role in increasing productivity. This has been amply proved by the experience of many countries and also by the use of high-yielding varieties of wheat in Punjab, Haryana and Western Uttar Pradesh in our own country. Farmers should also be educated in the methods of sowing, maturing and irrigating the new high-yielding varieties of seeds.

4) Irrigation:

Use of improved seeds and fertilizers require proper irrigation facilities. Irrigation can also make multiple cropping possible in a number of areas and hence enhance productivity.

5) Plant Protection:

Agricultural scientists have estimated that approximately 5 percent of the crops are damaged by insects, pests and diseases. Most of the farmers in the countryside are unaware of the medicines and insecticides developed in recent years to face this challenge posed by diseases and insects. The government should maintain its own technical staff to carry out the spraying of pesticides and insecticides.

6) Provision of Credit and Marketing Facilities:

Use of improved varieties of seeds, fertilizers, pesticides, insecticides, agricultural machinery and irrigation facilities, all require substantial money resources which small farmers do not usually possess. Therefore, it is necessary to strengthen the credit cooperative sector and free it from the clutches of large landowners. Total food grain production increased from 50.8 million tonnes in 1950-51 to 234.47 million tonnes in 2008-09. The production of food grains declined to 218.11 million tonnes during 2009 10 due to long spells of drought in various parts of the country in 2009.As per the second advance estimates released by Ministry of Agriculture on February 9, 2011, production of food grains during 2010-11 is estimated at 232.07 million tonnes compared to 218.11 million tonnes in 2009-10. In the non-food grains group, jute and cotton show slow progress. Oilseeds production increased from 12.7 million tonnes in 1987-88 to 24.7 million tonnes in 1998-99. It fell to 15.1 million tonnes in 2002-03 but then fluctuated around 25 million tonnes in further subsequent periods. A significant improvement in yield has resulted in an increased growth rate of cotton production from 2.80 per cent during the 1980s to 13.58 percent per annum during 2000-10.

7) **Proper Education:**
Positive efforts have been taken by the government to educate the illiterate poor farmers about the new methods of technical farming. All the marginal farmers and tillers must know how to introduce the latest scientific technology in the cultivable lands. This will increase productivity.

8) **Package Programme:**
Proper implementation of 'Package Programme (i.e. irrigation, high yielding variety seeds, chemical fertilizers, modern machineries etc.) is necessary to increase the productivity of the soil. The effects of the green revolution are huge. All these not only increase the fertility of land, but change the single time crop producing land into multi-production. In India most of the lands are unfertile and have no permanent water flowing system. Thus per hectare production is very poor. Therefore, the government has to take positive initiatives! Implements 'Package Programme' throughout every corner of the country. These will help to increase the fertility of the soil. According to agricultural scientists in India nearly 5% of the total crop production is destroyed by different insects, pests and diseases. Maximum farmers are ignorant about the use of insecticides and pesticides. Hence to increase productivity the government must take initiatives to start several programmes.

3.4. Scarcity of Capital:

Capital is considered as the most important factor in the development of an economy. In underdeveloped economies like India, capital availability per person is very low which results in low productivity and low per capita income. Low per capita income again results in low savings, low investment and low capital formation. Thus Underdeveloped Countries (UDCs) are caught in the grip of vicious circle of poverty. Lack of capital does not allow an economy to introduce the latest technologies. Thus, economy becomes technologically backward and internationally in competitive. The CSO's Quick Estimates for 2009-10 placed gross domestic savings at 33.7 percent of the GDP at current market prices. With private-sector savings more or less static, ii was the savings of the public sector that went up from a revised level of 0.5 percent in 2008-09 to 2.1 percent in 2009-10. In the investment sphere the ratio of gross investment came down to around 36.5 percent in 2009-10 from 38 percent in 2007-08. The basic economic problem that arises because people have unlimited wants but resources are limited. Because of scarcity, various economic decisions must be made to allocate resources efficiently.

3.4.1 Significance of Capital Formation:

Capital formation or accumulation is regarded as one of the important and principal factors in economic development. According to Nurkse, the vicious circles of poverty in underdeveloped countries can be broken through capital formation. Due to low levels of income in such countries, demand, production and investment are deficient. This results in the deficiency of capital goods which can be removed by capital formation. The supplies of machines equipment and tools increase. The scale of production expands. Social and economic overheads are created. It is capital formation that leads to the fuller utilisation of available resource. Thus capital formation leads to increase in the size of national output, income and employment thereby solving the problems of inflation and balance of payments, and making the economy free from the burden of foreign debts. We discuss below the importance of capital formation in detail.

1) **Formation of Economic and Social Overhead Capital:**
In the initial stages of economic development in underdeveloped countries, economic structure needs to construct in the form of buildings, roads, railways, hospitals and schools in great numbers as economic and social overhead capital which needs more capital. Hence, in under developed countries by the process of capital formation, the possibility of economic development gets more strength as for economic development depends in under-developed countries on the size and extent of the available necessary conditions in the country as in transport and economic and social security measures. In this way capital formation plays an important role in the formation and development of basic capital goods in underdeveloped countries.

2) **Technical Progress:**
Capital formation in underdeveloped countries creates overhead capital and necessary environment for economic development. This helps to instigate technical progress which makes possible the use of more capital in the field of production and with increase of capital in production, the abstract form of capital changes and mostly it is seen that present changes in the capital structure leads to changes in structure and size of technique and public is thereby more influenced. Technical progress has become a necessary condition for the present day economic progress and speed of economic progress depends on the rate of technical progress. Hence in underdeveloped countries for economic development to use modem techniques in production, it is necessary to increase the rate of capital formation as rate of technical progress depends on the rate of capital formation.

3) **Use of Round about Methods of Production:**
In underdeveloped countries process of capital formation makes possible the use of roundabout or complex methods of production which makes the division in different stages on the basis of modem techniques and production process leads to specialisation and rationalisation. This leads to rapid growth in production and in large scale. In this way by capital formation modem machines and instruments are utilized on the basis of modem techniques with cyclic method. This will lead to unexpected rise in productivity and economic development will be over strengthened.

4) Maximum Exploitation of General Resources:

In under-developed countries there is increase in the capacity of risk taking by capital formation by which fresh sources of natural resources are made available and is made possible the proper and thoughtful exploitation of natural resources. Besides extra capital formation exploits the economy in normal resources on the basis of modem techniques and divisional imbalances are prevented by finding new fields of natural resources. This is clear that rate of capital formation is dependent itself on natural and human resources but this is also true that utility and development of other sources of production are dependent on the rate of capital formation in the country.

5) Human Capital Formation:

Capital formation is important in the qualitative development of human resources. Human capital formation depends on the citizen's education, training, health, social and economic security, freedom and welfare facilities for which sufficient capital are needed. Besides labour force needs up-to-date implements and instruments in sufficient quantity so that with the increase of population there will be optimum increase in production and increased labour force is absorbed in the business. So capital formation has importance in the human capital formation so that labour force is given social and economic facilities with knowledge and skill.

6) Increase in National Income:

Capital formation improves the conditions and methods of production of a country. Hence, there is much increase in the national income, quantity and the rate. This leads to increase in quantity of production and rate of income per capita which leads to again rise in national income. Hence, the rate of growth and quantity of national income necessarily depends on the rate of capital formation. So increase in national income is possible only by the proper use of different means of production and productive use of capital formation.

7) Expansion of Economic Activities:

After the increase in the rate of capital formation, capital is more in the economy and productivity increases quickly and available capital is utilized in more profitable and extensive way. In this way, complicated techniques and methods are utilized for the economy and economic activities expand. As a result of capital formation, increase in investment effects economic development in two ways. On the one hand it increases the per capita income and enhances the purchasing power which in turn creates more effective demand in the economy while on the other hand investment leads to increase the production. Besides extended market helps vicious circles of poverty to break. Prof Nurkse has emphasized to break the vicious circles of poverty for increasing the investment and extension of market. In this way by capital formation, economic activities can be expanded in under-developed countries and so in turn productivity can be increased by which they can get rid of poverty and attain economic development.

8) **Decline in Dependence on Foreign Capital:**
In underdeveloped countries process of capital formation increases dependence on internal resources and domestic savings by which dependence on foreign capital is lessened. Economic development leaves burden of foreign capital hence to give interest on foreign capital and bear expenses of foreign scientists, country has to be burdened by improper taxation to the public. This gives setback to internal savings. In this way by capital formation only a country can attain self-sufficiency and can get rid of foreign capital's dependence.

9) **Increase in Economic Welfare:**
By the increase in rate of capital formation public are getting more facilities in economic and social field by which they are more benefited economically. Capital formation leads to unexpected increase in their productivity and income and this improves their standard of living. This leads to improvement and enhancement in the chances of work. Citizens avail of the faith for life expectance and social security resultant to economic activities and welfare of the people.

3.4.2 Reasons for Scarcity of Capital:

The following are the reasons for scarcity of capital:

1) **Poverty or Low Per-capita Income:**
A majority of people in the underdeveloped countries is poor. Various sectors of production, such as, industries, agriculture, transport, etc., are backward. So, the gross production is low. Saving, too, is very low. Low saving causes low rate of capital formation.

2) **More Population:**
Several underdeveloped countries have large population. One of its effects is that the rate of wages is low. Owing to low wages, savings cannot be made. As such the rate of capital formation remains low. Another effect of the sharp rise in population is that whatever development is made by these countries through government and private efforts or whatever increase is made in production, is consumed in providing subsistence to the growing population, and hence, cannot be used for capital formation.

3) **Inflation or Increase in Prices:**
A majority of the governments of the underdeveloped countries have to take to deficit financing so as to make up for the growing expenditure on economic development. As a result, there is a lot of increase in prices. Prices in India, too, have gone up due to deficit financing. Owing to price-rise, the public has to spend a big chunk of its income. As such, their capacity to save becomes low, and the rate of capital formation also becomes low.

4) **Demonstration Effect:**

Public expenditure increases and the rate of capital formation become low due to the demonstration effect in the underdeveloped countries. The affluent class starts spending money on imported luxury goods like tape recorder, watches, costly clothes, video, colour television etc. The low income group people imitate their way of life and start spending much of their income on expensive consumer durables. Consequently, expenditure increases, and saving becomes meager. As such, there is a low rate of capital formation.

5) **Less Facilities of Investment:**

For capital formation, it is essential to have the investment facilities along with savings. In the underdeveloped countries, the facilities for investment are limited. There is lack of able entrepreneurs banking institutions, modem techniques, etc., also in these countries. Low investment means less capital formation.

6) **Increase in Taxes:**

Taxation system of the government, too, affects the capital formation adversely in the underdeveloped countries. In these countries, direct taxes like, income tax, etc., are very progressive. Taxation rates increase as income increases. As a result, a major portion of income is used to pay the taxes. Thus, the disposable income of the taxpayers becomes low. Consequently, their saving capacity also becomes low. The rates of indirect taxes like, sales tax and excise duty in these countries are also high. These taxes cause price hike. Spending of the people goes up and savings go down. Low savings result in low capital formation.

7) **Lack of Financial Institutions:**

It is essential for capital formation that private saving is mobilized and the people are given facilities to make small saving. For this purpose, it important to have large number of financial institutions, especially in the rural areas of the country. Such institutions are lacking in the underdeveloped countries. As a result, private saving is not adequately mobilized and the entrepreneurs are unable to get adequate credit facilities, at reasonable rate of interest, keeping the level of investment low.

8) **Limited Extent of Market:**

People in the underdeveloped countries have low purchasing power and low demand. So, the extent of market is limited. Owing to the limited extent of market, production is also low. Low production means low income, low employment, low saving and low investment. Therefore, lack of demand, too is a major factor behind the lack of capital formation in these countries.

9) **Lack of Able Entrepreneur:**

Most of the people, in under developed countries, are employed in business, services, subsistence agriculture and cottage industries. Large scale industries being highly capital intensive requires huge capital investment. These industries are not established in the absence of able and competent entrepreneurs and shortage of capital. As such, investment is low and capital formation also remains low.

10) Lack of Overhead Capital:

In the underdeveloped countries, overhead capital like transport, electricity, communications, banking, social services etc., are insufficient. Due to their inadequacy, agriculture and industries cannot develop. So, the rate of capital formation is low.

11) Labour Intensive Technique:

Agriculture, in the underdeveloped countries is in a backward state. Supply of labour being large, labour intensive techniques is mostly used in these countries. As a result, demand for capital is also very low.

12) Low Productivity:

The productivity of the workers in the underdeveloped countries is low due to illiteracy, ill-health, low wages, low level of technical skill, etc. As such, their income is low, and they cannot affect savings. The rate of capital formation remains low for want of savings.

13) Unequal Distribution of Income and Wealth:

On account of unequal distribution of wealth and income in under developed countries, large section of the population has no capacity to save. It also accounts for low capital formation.

3.4.3 Suggestions to Increase the Rate of Capital Formation:

Following are some suggestions for achieving this:

1) Tax Result:

The taxation policy should be revised and adequate tax reliefs should be allowed to salaried persons and industrialists.

2) Encourage Savings:

Steps should be taken to intensify and motivate small savings, for which rate of interest on savings should be attractive. Saving schemes like (P.F.) provident fund, compulsory insurance, compulsory deposits, etc., should be encouraged and extended.

3) Facilitate Investment and Production:

Many more avenues of investment and production should be increased by establishing and implementing schemes in agriculture, industry, transport, banking, insurance, trade, etc.

4) Maintenance of Law and Order:

The law and order condition in every part of the country should be improved and security of life and property must be ensured.

5) Equal Distribution of Wealth:

There should be a proper distribution of wealth.

6) Improving and Developing Basic Utilities:

General facilities like means of transportation, communication, power plants, ports, technical training facilities, etc., should be improved and developed in an adequate way.

7) Cheap Capital:

The investors avail credits from various agencies for their growth, but the rates of interest at which credit is available to them is high, thus increasing the cost of capital results in low profit margins for investors. A lower rate of interest will increase the profit and stimulate investments.

8) Identification of Investments:

The productive investments should be encouraged but unproductive investments should not be entertained.

3.5. Inappropriate Technology:

Inappropriate technology has many definitions which range from strictly technical (equipment which is technically unsuitable to the conditions of its operation) to highly political (e.g., equipment manufactured in the "wrong" country or by the "wrong" type of company).

3.5.1 Role of Technology in Economic Development:

Technology encompasses a huge body of knowledge and tools that ease the use of economic resources as a way to produce goods and services efficiently and innovatively. Technological progress is essential to economic growth and development, and the more advanced the technology available, the more quickly the local and global economy can improve. Technology equipment and services for the production of economic resources or technologies that facilitate learning. Adoption of technology leads to higher income, ample capital resources, supported by good management and technical skills. Role of Technology in economic development is as below.

1) Increase in Labor Productivity:

With labor productivity growth in the use of technology. If we help the agricultural sector, for example, a farmer with tractor can work more than ten farmers.

2) More Human Capital:

Human capital means skilled and educated labor force when we increase the use of technology the skills in labor also increase; it leads to human capital formation.

3) Providing Better Living Standard:

We enjoy living facilities per capita income and the quality of life decision. Technology, national income and per capita income growth using, is it leads to better quality of life.

4) Output Increases:

As labor productivity increases the production level increase of country. This cause increase in national income of a country.

5) Rapid increase in supply:

According to Keynes rapid increase in supply is possible with the help of technology. If demand of a commodity increase, it is possible to match the demand with the help of technology. It removes the danger of inflation.

6) Trade:

The basis of international trade is "a country exchanges its excess production with the excess production of another country". So with the use of technology production and international trade also increase.

7) Advancement in Infrastructure:

Technology itself is the component of infrastructure with the use of advancement in technology we can improve .such as use of atomic energy, use of gas in place of petrol, and computer etc.

8) No Wastages of Resources:

Technology helps in removing wastages of resources in production. It is possible to have more output with same inputs in the presence of technology.

9) Cost Minimizing:

According to the Gallbraith "The increasing use of technology in a society as the efficiency increases. Growth of national income and expense control in results

10) Economics of Scale:

It means that advantages are attached with high production level.in this modern era we know that the use of technology production will increase as a result cost will decrease and profit will increase.

11) Overcome Vicious Circle of Poverty:

With the use of technology income of the country increase. When increase in income saving will increase , demand will increase and as a result investment and capital formation will increase that help to overcome the vicious circle of poverty.

12) Improvement of Quality:

When we use latest technology in the production of new goods then their quality of product will improve. If we take the example of textile industry the quality of machine made cloth is better than the quality of handmade clothes. And their production will be more.

13) Useful Labor Force:

Skilled labor can also be used for more production. If labor will be highly skilled than they know how to use the machines effectively. That can also be profitable for the country and industry.

3.5.2 Problems of Inappropriate Technology:

The use of inappropriate technology in various sectors can lead to a range of problems and inefficiencies.

1) Low Productivity:
Inappropriate technology may lack the efficiency and effectiveness required to maximize productivity. Outdated or inefficient machinery, tools, or processes can result in low output, increased labor requirements, and suboptimal resource utilization.

2) High Operational Costs:
Inappropriate technology can lead to higher operational costs. This may be due to inefficient energy consumption, excessive maintenance requirements, or the need for skilled labor that is in short supply. High operational costs can reduce profitability and hinder the growth and competitiveness of businesses.

3) Environmental Impact:
Technology that is not environmentally friendly can contribute to pollution, resource depletion, and ecological damage. Inadequate waste management systems, excessive energy consumption, and harmful emissions can have adverse effects on ecosystems and human health.

4) Safety and Health Risks:
Inappropriate technology can pose safety and health risks to workers and users. This may be due to inadequate safety features, poor ergonomics, or exposure to hazardous substances. Unsafe working conditions can result in accidents, injuries, and long-term health problems.

5) Limited Adaptability:
Technology that is not adaptable or flexible can become obsolete quickly or fail to meet evolving needs. In rapidly changing industries or environments, the inability to upgrade or adapt technology may hinder competitiveness and innovation.

6) Inequality and Exclusion:
Inappropriate technology can perpetuate social and economic inequalities. When technologies are not accessible or affordable for marginalized communities or regions, it can widen the digital divide and hinder opportunities for development and social inclusion.

7) Cultural and Social Disruption:
Technology that does not consider local cultural, social, and behavioral contexts can lead to disruptions and resistance. It may disregard traditional practices, erode local livelihoods, and undermine community cohesion.

8) Limited Local Capacity Development:
Reliance on inappropriate technology may hinder the development of local skills, knowledge, and innovation. When technology is imported without consideration for

local expertise and capacity building, it can hinder the development of a skilled workforce and inhibit local innovation.

3.5.3 Suggestions for Technology Development:

Here are some suggestions for technology development:

1) **Investment in Research and Development (R&D):**
Governments, private sector organizations, and international institutions should prioritize investment in R&D activities. This includes allocating funding, creating incentives for innovation, and establishing research institutions and partnerships. R&D efforts should target key sectors such as agriculture, healthcare, energy, and information technology.

2) **Collaboration and Knowledge Sharing:**
Encouraging collaboration between industry, academia, and research institutions is crucial for technology development. Creating platforms for knowledge sharing, fostering networks, and supporting public-private partnerships can facilitate the exchange of ideas, expertise, and resources.

3) **Support for Startups and Entrepreneurship:**
Providing support and resources for startups and entrepreneurs can stimulate technological innovation. This includes access to funding, incubation programs, mentorship, and networking opportunities. Governments can create favorable policies, regulatory frameworks, and tax incentives to promote startup ecosystems and technology entrepreneurship.

4) **Education and Skill Development:**
Promoting science, technology, engineering, and mathematics (STEM) education is essential for nurturing a skilled workforce and fostering technology development. Enhancing technical and vocational training programs, establishing innovation hubs, and incorporating technology-focused curricula can develop a talent pool capable of driving technological advancements.

5) **Intellectual Property Rights Protection:**
Ensuring strong intellectual property rights protection is crucial to incentivize innovation and technology development. Implementing effective patent systems, copyright laws, and mechanisms to protect intellectual property rights can encourage investment in research and the commercialization of technologies.

6) **Collaboration with International Institutions:**
Engaging with international institutions, such as the World Intellectual Property Organization (WIPO) and the World Trade Organization (WTO), can facilitate technology transfer, access to funding, and knowledge sharing. Collaboration with international partners can accelerate technology development through joint research projects, technology sharing, and capacity building initiatives.

7) **Infrastructure Development:**
Investing in infrastructure development, such as broadband internet connectivity, power grids, and research facilities, is essential for technology development. Reliable and affordable access to infrastructure supports the adoption and utilization of technology across various sectors.

8) **Regulatory Support and Policies:**
Governments should develop supportive policies and regulations that foster technology development. This includes creating an enabling environment for innovation, streamlining bureaucratic processes, and providing incentives for technology adoption and commercialization. Policies that promote sustainability, environmental protection, and social inclusion should also be prioritized.

9) **Technology Transfer and Adaptation:**
Facilitating technology transfer from developed countries to developing countries can help bridge the technology gap. Encouraging technology transfer through partnerships, licensing agreements, and knowledge exchange programs can promote the adoption and adaptation of proven technologies to local contexts.

10) **Monitoring and Evaluation:**
Establishing mechanisms for monitoring and evaluating technology development initiatives can provide valuable insights and guide future strategies. Monitoring progress, measuring impact, and learning from successes and failures can help refine approaches and ensure the effectiveness and sustainability of technology development efforts.

3.6. Socio-Cultural Constraints:

Socio-cultural rigidities are another type of obstacles to economic development of underdeveloped countries. Rapid economic growth requires a particular attitude of mind and highly elastic institutional pattern. A sharp desire for material betterment, a willingness to work hard and in a regular and punctual manner, an awareness of the future benefits of present sacrifices are a pre-requisite to economic growth. But they are largely absent in underdeveloped countries and hence in many of them a social and cultural revolution is required while the industrial revolution is getting under way. According to U.N.O. Experts, "The people of a country must desire progress and their social, economic, legal and political institutions must be favourable to it." Prof. Nurkse also feels that economic development has much to do with human endowments, social attitudes, political conditions and historical accidents. Robert Gamer, a former Vice President of World Bank believes that: "Economic development or lack of it is primarily due to differences of people in their attitude, customs, traditions and the consequent differences in their political, social and religious institutions". The Socio-cultural patterns and the institutional structure in under developed countries are not conducive to change. In these countries there is lack of preparation for an industrial revolution. Not only that their agricultural and commercial sectors have not developed to the extent where they can support rapid industrial progress, but there has been little or no time for their institutions and value systems to adapt themselves to modem economic change. Thus there has been immense socio-economic hurdle to rapid economic development in these countries.

3.6.1 Socio-Cultural Values and Development:

Because sociocultural values influence how we, as people in society, interact with the world, they also influence how we approach the process of economic development. Some sociocultural values that can impact economic development include:

1) **Materialism** is the tendency to place greater value on physical needs or belongings than quality of life and spirituality. Post-materialism places greater value on spiritual well-being, quality of life, and relationships. Societies high in materialism are most likely to seek greater economic development in order to have more physical belongings. In contrast, post-materialist societies focus on enjoying the life available to them. Importantly, post-materialist societies are most likely to be identified in countries that are already developed and their material needs have been met.
2) **Collectivism** is a value that leads people to act for the greater good of the entire population, while individualism suggests that people should make decisions for their own benefit, since maximizing individual happiness is the best way to maximize societal happiness. In collectivist societies, activities that lead to economic development should benefit the majority, if not all, of the population. However, in individualist societies, one person is concerned about their own satisfaction and economic development often with little or no regard for the well-being of the greater society.
3) **Innovation** considers how interested a culture is in progress. Cultures high on innovation are excited and interested in new technologies, changes to society, and ultimately, economic growth. In contrast, cultures low on innovation may be fearful or hesitant to implement anything new into their society.
4) The values taught within religion influence how individuals approach everyday activities. In turn, these values and beliefs can influence personal decisions on work, business ventures, and industrialization.
5) **Obedience** refers to how much citizens conform to the social norms and expectations. High obedience means that decisions made are in line with the cultural norms, and people are discouraged from doing anything outside of these norms.
6) **Thrift**, or frugality, refers to how much the culture saves money and sees value in saving money. Some cultures are focused on saving and not spending, while others are more interested in investment and making profit. Because economic development requires both saving and spending, the level of thrift and practices of spending within the culture can have an important impact on further development.

7) And finally, **risk propensity** is the level of risk an individual is naturally inclined to accept. Cultures high in risk propensity are more likely to accept the unknown, such as a new business venture, than those low in risk propensity.

3.6.2 Role of Socio-Cultural Factors:

Socio-cultural factors play a significant role in economic development as they shape the values, beliefs, norms, and behaviors of individuals and communities within a society. These factors can either facilitate or hinder economic progress. Here are some ways in which socio-cultural factors influence economic development:

1) **Work Ethic and Entrepreneurship:**
The cultural values and beliefs surrounding work, entrepreneurship, and innovation can impact economic development. Societies that value hard work, entrepreneurship, and risk-taking tend to have higher levels of economic productivity and innovation. Conversely, cultures that discourage risk-taking or prioritize leisure over work may hinder economic development.

2) **Social Capital and Trust:**
Social capital refers to the networks, relationships, and trust among individuals and social groups. Strong social capital can foster economic development by facilitating cooperation, trade, and investment. Trustworthy institutions, reliable business networks, and a sense of social cohesion contribute to economic growth by reducing transaction costs and facilitating economic activities.

3) **Gender Roles and Women's Empowerment:**
The status and roles assigned to women within a society have a profound impact on economic development. Societies that promote gender equality, provide opportunities for women's education, and enable their participation in the workforce tend to experience higher levels of economic growth and development. Women's empowerment is linked to improved productivity, poverty reduction, and social well-being.

4) **Cultural Attitudes toward Saving and Investment:**
Cultural attitudes and beliefs toward saving, investment, and financial management can influence economic development. Cultures that emphasize long-term planning, savings, and investment tend to have higher levels of capital accumulation and investment in productive activities, leading to economic growth. In contrast, cultures that prioritize immediate consumption may hinder savings and investment rates.

5) **Education and Human Capital:**
Education is a critical socio-cultural factor that influences economic development. Cultures that value and prioritize education tend to have higher levels of human capital, which is crucial for economic productivity, innovation, and technological advancement. Accessible and quality education can enhance individuals' skills, knowledge, and capabilities, contributing to economic growth.

6) **Cultural Attitudes toward Risk and Innovation:**
Cultural attitudes toward risk-taking, innovation, and experimentation influence economic development. Societies that are open to change, tolerate failure, and encourage innovation tend to have more dynamic and entrepreneurial economies. Conversely, cultures that are resistant to change or fear failure may hinder economic progress and innovation.

7) **Cultural Acceptance of Diversity and Inclusion:**
Societies that embrace diversity, tolerate differences, and promote inclusivity tend to foster economic development. Inclusive societies encourage participation, collaboration, and the exchange of ideas from diverse perspectives, leading to innovation, creativity, and economic growth.

8) **Cultural Norms and Corruption:**
Cultural norms and attitudes toward corruption can have a significant impact on economic development. Cultures that reject corruption, promote transparency, and value ethical behavior tend to have more efficient institutions, better governance, and higher levels of economic development. In contrast, cultures that tolerate or accept corruption can hinder economic progress by distorting markets, reducing investment, and undermining public trust.

3.6.3 Socio-Cultural Factors affected Development:

Following socio-cultural factors are affected development:

1) **Discrimination:**
Sometimes there are social or cultural factors that hold back poor countries. Discrimination is one of these. If there are certain people groups that are discriminated against, the country's overall productivity can suffer. This may be a tribe, a caste, a racial category or minority language group. I have already mentioned Cameroon, which has both French speaking and English speaking regions. The entire infrastructure happens in the French speaking part. French speakers in Canada complain of the opposite. Welsh speakers in Britain, or Catalans in Spain, have historically faced similar problems.

Racial discrimination may be an issue, excluding certain groups from economic activity, either deliberately or not. Racial minorities regularly have poorer exam results and economic prospects than the majority. More serious forms of exclusion would be apartheid South Africa, or the Asian communities driven out of Uganda under Idi Amin, which was disastrous for Uganda's economy. This racial discrimination is international too. The old 'whites in charge' power structures of colonialism might be formally gone and old colonies now independent – but they cast a long shadow. Global power is still very much tilted towards the northern hemisphere.

Another division may be the role of women. Jeffrey Sachs talks about this in The End of Poverty: 'Cultural or religious norms may block the role of women… leaving half the population without economic or political rights and without education, thereby undermining half of the population in its contribution to overall development.' If you don't believe that women should work, you have effectively halved the earning potential of your country.

2) Population:

Closely linked to the role of women is the population issue. If women see staying at home and bringing up children as their primary role, they will often have more children than those who work. This is not necessarily a problem, but fewer children can bring benefits for development. Jeffrey Sachs again: 'With fewer children, a poor household can invest more in the health and education of each child, thereby equipping the next generation with the health, nutrition, and education that can lift living standards in future years.'

In the last century, the world's population grew dramatically. What is interesting is that the countries where this has happened are often those where women do not play a role in business or society. When women are educated and given a choice, some will stay at home and look after children, and others will pursue careers or start small businesses. This is an important factor, as some countries have seen their population double or triple without their economies keeping pace. That leaves more mouths to feed, and just not enough to go around. The answers lie in access to family planning, and in the empowering of women and girls so that everyone can make a good decision for themselves and their families.

3) Culture:

We already mentioned the role of women, but culture can have hidden effects in business, trade and development. China may be a major power now, but it was the world's most developed country in the middle ages. It stagnated, or even went backwards, for centuries. Part of this was cultural, a pride and sense of self-sufficiency that led to a closing of China's borders. 'China seems to have long been stationary', Adam Smith wrote in 1776, in his Wealth of Nations. 'A country which neglects or despises foreign commerce… cannot transact the same quantity of business which it might do with different laws and institutions.' That's changed, but nationalism, suspicion, or radical philosophy still has some countries closed down to outside involvement – communism in North Korea, or extremist Islam in Taliban Afghanistan, locking countries out of development.

This the far end of the spectrum, but culture works in subtler ways too. Some cultures believe in a greater good, in unity, in the rule of law. They are optimistic, hopeful, ambitious and ready to pull together. Others can be paranoid, fragmented, uncertain of their place in the modern world, angry, resistant to change. Rich countries can be overconfident and brash. Poor countries can see themselves as victims and become despondent. In his The Wealth and Poverty of Nations, economic historian David Landes says 'If we learn anything from the history of economic development it is that culture makes all the difference.'

4) The Limits of Cultural Interpretations:

At the same time, cultural influences on development are notoriously hard to call from the outside. Hinduism was often cited as one of the reasons why India would never develop. Because everyone accepts their place in the world, it was assumed that Hindus would lack the ambition required to innovate and do business on an international stage. The recent growth in India's economy proves that wrong quite spectacularly. Korean economist Ha-Joon Chang quotes a 1911 travel book that describes Koreans as "sullen, lazy and religionless savages", something that hardly holds true today. So did Korean culture change, or was the writer simply being superior? Making assumptions about other cultures has at times been a tool of colonialism and oppression. In the days of empire, the British believed they were superior to other cultures and that it was in everybody's interests for them to be in charge. In fact, it was their duty to take charge and 'civilise' cultures that were seen as 'savage' or primitive. All kinds of racism and abuse were legitimised this way.

3.7. Political and Administrative Constraints:

For accelerating the rate of economic development, there should be political stability in the country. If there is a change in the government set up due to elections, or of dictatorship, the planning job done by the previous government should not be altered altogether. The planning machinery and all others involved in administration should be loyal to the country. They should be competent sympathetic and honest in the performance of the duties assigned to them. In Pakistan, since its inception, there are rapid changes in governments. Each government which came into power condemned the planning work done by the previous governments. They framed their own plans, formulated their own strategies of development and left the claim without achieving the targets of the Plans. The history of planning shows that with the exception of the Faith Five Year Plan, all other Plans have failed to achieve their targets. The overall line of the planning machinery in Pakistan is bureaucratic rather than professional. The administration working in various departments is generally weak, incompetent and unsympathetic. Self-interest is dominating over national interest which is a great barrier to economic development. Another administrative obstacle line the way of economic development is that we have not so far been able to decide about the nature of economic system to be adopted in Pakistan. Mixed economy, Socialistic economy. Islamic economy all are talked about but nothing concrete has actually been practiced. There should be clarity on this fundamental issue so that planning is drawn up according to the socio-economic objective of that system and a path of development lay out. In most of the developing countries, the governments are not stable. A new government comes into power overnight; either through coup defeat or army takes over. The new government introduces a new system of rules for the operation of business which causes frustration and discontentment among the people. How political instability affect growth does is discussed in brief below.

3.7.1 Influence of Political Instability:

When there is lack of political stability in the country, it directly affects economic growth. It closes off sources of internal and external investments.

1) **The External Investors:**
   The external investors do not invest in a country where there is political instability. The flow of investment in countries where there is civil war coups, army take over etc. is either negligible or zero.
2) **Internal Investment:**
   Political instability also limits internal investment. The wealthy class in developing countries has enough income to spare. They can invest their savings in profitable projects. Generally, they avoid investing founds in their own country for fear of nationalization of their projects, large scale interference by militant trade unions, harsh and exploitative attitude of the various govt. agencies involved in the setting and operation of the projects etc. The well off people including the politicians in developing countries prefers to take their money outside the country or channel their investment out of their own country. The developing countries are therefore, deprived of investment funds which adversely affect economic growth.
3) **Internal Disorder:**
   The defeated political parties, the rich landlords, the various ethnic groups etc. who are not able to capture power take up and support anti govt. activities by taking out processions, making bomb blasts, killing the innocent people by indiscriminate firing etc. All these activities result in creating political instability in the country and as such adversely affect economic development.

3.7.2 Political Obstacles in Economic Development:

The following are the different political obstacles in economic development:

1) **Lack of Administrative Skills:**
   Government support is essential to economic development. Whether support means allowing private enterprise to flourish and develop or actively managing the allocation of resources, a poorly organised or corrupt government can present an obstacle to economic growth. Some developing countries have suffered from well-meaning but inept government management. This is most obvious in countries with a long history of cannibalization. For example, when the Democratic Republic of the

Congo won independence from Belgium, few of its native citizens were college educated. Moreover, Belgians had run most of the important government offices. Independence brought a large group of inexperienced and unskilled workers to important positions of power. At first there was a period of "learning by doing."

2) **Political Instability and Risk:**
One of the most important functions that a government performs in stimulating economic growth is providing a political environment that encourages saving and investment. People do not want to do business in an economy that has been weakened by wars, demonstrations, or uncertainty. For instance, since becoming an independent nation in 1825, Bolivia has had more than 150 changes in government. This kind of instability forces citizens to take a short-run view of the economy. Long-term planning is impossible when people do not know what the attitudes and policies of the government that is going to be in power next year or even next month will be.

3) **Corruption:**
Corrupt practices by government officials have long reduced economic growth. Payment of money or gifts in order to receive a government service or benefit is quite widespread in many countries. Research shows that there is a definite negative relationship between the level of corruption in a country and both investment and growth.

4) **Good Economics as Bad Politics:**
Every Third World politician wants to maximize economic growth, all things being equal. But all things are rarely equal. Political pressures may force a government to work toward more immediate objectives than economic growth.

3.8. External Bottlenecks:

The economic development criteria are identical for developing countries and countries with advanced economies. Both must use their existing supplies of resources more efficiently and must also increase their available supplies of resources, although all developing countries are aware of these criteria for economic development, the economic, institutional, and cultural conditions in these nations are the reasons why they experience different rates of economic growth. Consider the following external bottleneck to economic development in developing countries.

1) **Human Resources in Developing Countries:**
Developing countries tend to be overpopulated and have high rates of population growth. These growing populations decrease the developing countries' capacities to save, invest, and increase productivity. Developing countries often experience both high levels of unemployment and underemployment.

2) **Shortages of Capital Goods:**
Developing countries generally have shortages of capital goods such as public utilities, machinery, and factories. These shortages stem from a lack of saving and

investment because the nations are too poor to save. Insufficient amounts of capital goods contribute to low levels of labor productivity. Moreover, technological advancement is slow in developing countries, which retards economic development.

3) **Non-Diversified Economies:**
The economies of many developing countries are non-diversified, and emphasize the production of primary products such as bauxite, copper, and agricultural goods. Developing countries would generally prefer to diversify their economies by fostering manufacturing industries.

4) **Hinder Economic Development:**
Besides economic factors, institutional and cultural factors can hinder economic development. **For example**, political corruption and bribery are common in many developing countries. Also, economic growth depends partly on the desire to develop. The people in developing countries willing to make the necessary changes in their ways of doing things in order to promote growth.

5) **International Trade Barriers:**
Trade barriers, such as tariffs, quotas, and non-tariff barriers, can hinder a country's ability to participate in global trade and access international markets. Restrictions on imports and exports can limit a country's economic growth potential, hamper competitiveness, and restrict access to vital resources and technology.

6) **Limited Market Access:**
Inadequate access to international markets due to geographical factors, lack of transportation infrastructure, or trade restrictions can hamper economic development. Limited market access limits opportunities for export-led growth, reduces economies of scale, and hinders the integration of domestic industries into global value chains.

7) **Capital Constraints:**
Limited access to capital from international financial markets can hinder economic development. Developing countries may face difficulties in accessing affordable external financing for investments in infrastructure, technology, and human capital development. High borrowing costs, limited credit availability, and volatile international capital flows can restrict investment and impede economic growth.

8) **Technology Gap:**
Technological disparities between countries can act as an external bottleneck for economic development. Limited access to advanced technology and inadequate capacity for technology transfer can hinder innovation, productivity growth, and competitiveness. Technological gaps can limit a country's ability to catch up with more technologically advanced nations.

9) **Natural Disasters and Climate Change:**
Natural disasters, such as earthquakes, floods, hurricanes, and droughts, can disrupt economic activities, destroy infrastructure, and lead to economic setbacks.

Climate change-related impacts, including rising sea levels, extreme weather events, and changing rainfall patterns, can exacerbate vulnerability and hinder long-term economic development efforts.

10) Dependency on Primary Commodities:

Dependence on the export of primary commodities, such as agricultural products or raw materials, can expose economies to external shocks and price volatility. Fluctuations in commodity prices can lead to revenue instability, hinder diversification efforts, and impede sustainable economic growth.

11) Political Instability and Conflict:

Political instability, social unrest, and armed conflicts can severely hamper economic development. These factors create an uncertain and volatile environment that deters investment, disrupts production, undermines infrastructure, and hinders the implementation of sound economic policies.

12) Global Economic Cycles:

Global economic cycles, including recessions and financial crises, can have a significant impact on developing economies. Economic downturns in major economies can lead to reduced demand for exports, reduced investment flows, and disruptions in global financial markets, which can adversely affect economic development efforts.

Review Questions

Q. 2. Answer in 100 Words:

1) State the Causes of Vicious Circle of Poverty.
2) Explain the Suggestions to Increase the Rate of Capital Formation.
3) State the Stages of Population Explosion.
4) Explain the Problems Due to Over Population Explosion.
5) Write about the Influence of Political Instability.
6) State the Measures of Low Productivity of Agriculture.

Q. 3. Answer in 200 Words:

1) Explain in detail Measures to Control Vicious Circle of Poverty
2) Discuss the Significance of Capital Formation.
3) Explain the Reasons for Scarcity of Capital.
4) State the Role of Technology in Economic Development.
5) Discuss the Socio-Cultural Values and Development.
6) Suggestions for Population Explosion.
7) Explain the Problems of Low Productivity of Agriculture.

Q. 4. Answer in 400 Words:

1) What is Vicious Circle of Poverty? Explain the Causes and Measures of Vicious Circle of Poverty.
2) State the Causes of Low Productivity of Agriculture.
3) Discuss in detail about the Capital Constraints Development Process.
4) Explain the Technological Constraints in Development Process.
5) State the Socio-Cultural Constraints in Development Process.
6) Discuss the Political and Administrative Obstacles in Economic Development.
7) State the External Bottlenecks in Development Process.
8) Explain the Problems of Inappropriate Technology

Q.4 Write Short Note on Following:

1) Vicious Circle of Poverty.
2) Population Explosion.
3) Low Productivity of Agriculture.
4) External Bottlenecks.
5) Suggestions for Technology Development.

❖❖❖❖❖❖❖❖❖

Theories of Economic Development

UNIT 4

Introduction:

Growth and Development are importance factors of Economics.Economic development ideally refers to the sustained, concerted actions of communities and policymakers that improve the standard of living and economic health of a specific locality. The definition of economic development given by Professor Michael Todaro is an increase in living conditions, improvement of the citizens self-esteem needs and free and a just society. He suggests that the most accurate method of measuring economic development is the Human Development Index which takes into account the literacy rates & life expectancy which in-turn has an outright impact on productivity and could lead to Economic Growth. However, economic development can also be measured by taking into account the GDI (gender related index). Economic development can also be referred to as the quantitative and qualitative changes in an existing economy. Economic development involves development of human capital, increasing the literacy ratio, improve important infrastructure, improvement of health and safety and others areas that aims at increasing the general welfare of the citizens. The terms economic development and economic growth are used interchangeably but there is a very big difference between the two. Economic growth can be viewed as a sub category of economic development. Economic development is a government policy to increase the economic, social welfare and ensuring a stable political environment. Economic growth on the other hand is the general increase in the country products and services output.

4.1 Adam Smith's Theory of Economic Development:

Adam Smith, often referred to as the father of modern economics, laid the foundation for the theory of economic development through his seminal work "The Wealth of Nations," published in 1776. Smith's ideas and principles continue to shape economic thought and have had a profound impact on economic development theory. In following discussion we will explore Adam Smith's theory of economic development, covering key concepts such as the division of labor, market forces, and the role of government, among others.

4.1.1 Key Elements of Smith's Theory:

Adam Smith's theory of economic development is rooted in the notion that the wealth of nations is derived from the productivity and efficiency of its labor force. He argued that a nation's economic progress is driven by the division of labor, specialization, and the operation of market forces. Let's delve into the key elements of Smith's theory:

The main points of theory are as under:

1) **Capital Accumulation:**
   Accumulation of capital is the central point around which Adam Smith's theory of economic development revolves. The problem before the classical economists was how to increase the wealth of a country? The increase in wealth was considered as an index of country's prosperity. According to Adam Smith, the only way to increase wealth is to produce more, which in turn requires more capital investments. For this purpose, we must produce more capital. To produce more capital we must save more. Adam Smith therefore stressed the role of parsimoney, which formed the basis of capital accumulation. In order to practice parsimoney we should spend less of enjoyments for the sake of the future wants and enjoyments. The production and source of more capital is the integral part of capitalistic development of an economy. Thus capital accumulation is the central point of Adam Smith's theory of economic development."

2) **Production Technique:**
   Adam Smith recognised division of labour as a very important technique of production. It is division of labour that largely improves the productivity of labour. As a matter of fact, division of labour is the starting point of Smith's theory of economic growth. To him, division of labour was a very important technique to increase productivity, as it had increased the skill of every worker, saved the time to produce things, and promoted largely the inventions of labour-saving machines. In his opinion, the site of the market is an important limitation of the division of labour. Thus, this technique of production is useful and important, provided there is adequate market for the commodities and services produced.

3) **Agents of Economic Growth:**
   Adam Smith recognised farmers, producers and businessmen as the three significant agents of economic growth. He conceded that the free trade and open

market competition had led farmers, producers and businessmen to expand the markets, both domestic and international, which, in turn, had stimulated economic development so rapidly. To him, agriculture and industry along with commerce were fully complementary to each other. The agricultural surplus as a result of economic development enhances the demand for goods and services on the one hand and leads to rise in commercial progress and manufacturing industries on the other, which, in turn, leads to increase in the agricultural production through the utilisation of advanced techniques of production.

4) **Natural Law:**

Adam Smith advocated the philosophy of free and independent action. Freedom of action brings out the best of an individual which increases society's wealth and individual's desire to earn income in the manner he likes best. He advocated the operation of "Natural Law". Natural law was superior to the law of a state. Statutory law or the man-made law can never be 'perfect' whereas the natural law is perfect and beneficial for the society. Man should respect nature's law because nature law is just and moral. Nature teaches man the lesson of morality and honesty. These qualities exercise favourable effects on economic progress of the society.

5) **Laissez-Faire:**

Adam Smith's theory is based on the principle of laissez faire, which requires that state should not impose restrictions on individual's freedom of action. The policy of laissez faire would allow the producers ·to produce as much as they like, earn as much income as they can and save as much as they like. So the policy of laisseze-faire was considered as driving force for promoting growth variables such as saving, investment etc. Adam Smith believed that it was always safe to leave the economy to be propelled, regulated and controlled by the "invisible" hand i.e., the forces of competition motivated by self-interest be allowed to play their part in maximising the volume of savings of development.

6) **Free Trade:**

Trading is an essential concomitant of division of labour. The producers should be free to sell the produce whenever and wherever they like. The government should not interfere with the decisions of the business community.

7) **Trade Cycles:**

Adam Smith is of the view that the economic development is neither a smooth and simple affairs nor it is a sudden and abrupt process. He has an idea of "cumulative growth". Once development starts it proceeds in a cumulative manner. During the upswing phase every development variable moves in the upward direction i.e., saving, capital accumulation, employment, wages, income and demand, rise. The market expands and absorbs the increased production. The way economic development expands and growth variables continue multiplying, economy makes rapid strides till it enters the stage of "tale off". But the process of expansion does not continue forever. There are certain ceilings to the expansion possibilities and these have been recognised by Adam Smith. A stage is reached where the process of an upward tendency comes to a halt. The reason is that increase in the national output is eaten away by the growth of population. Declining marginal efficiency of capital disheartens the business community and investors are slackened, National output, wages, etc. move downwards. This leads to almost stationary and stagnant economy. Adam Smith has not suggested any way out of this stationary state. In short, Smith's ideas on economic development can be summed up as under. '

a) The main determinant of economic growth is capital formation which is considered as engine of development.

b) Capital-accumulation depends upon savings that is the differences between income and consumption.

c) Laissez-faire policy helps in maximising the output and savings.

d) Division of labour and specilisation increases the productivity of labour and widens the extent of market and trade. These are concomitants of economic growth.

e) Economic development is not a sudden or abrupt process; it is a gradual and cumulative process leading to the emergence of a stationary state. Smith's theory fails to provide scientific explanation for the process of development, yet his ideas about development have exercised a profound influence on the subsequent classical and neo-classical writers. However what has been said by Smith was primarily in the context of British economy with its emphasis on free economy.

4.1.2 Critics on Smith's Theory:

Adam Smith's theory of economic development has been widely influential and forms the basis of classical economics. However, like any economic theory, it has not been without its critics. In this response, I will explore some of the criticisms that have been leveled against Adam Smith's theory of economic development.

1) Oversimplification of Human Behavior:

One common criticism of Smith's theory is that it assumes individuals are solely motivated by self-interest and rational decision-making. Critics argue that human behavior is more complex and multifaceted, and factors such as social norms, cultural values, and altruism also influence economic decisions. Smith's focus on self-interest may overlook other important motivations that shape economic behavior.

2) Neglect of Income Distribution and Inequality:

Critics argue that Smith's theory pays little attention to income distribution and the potential for widening income inequality. While Smith recognized the importance of an efficient market system, he did not address the potential negative consequences of income disparities. In reality, unchecked market forces can lead to unequal distribution of wealth, social tensions, and reduced social mobility.

3) **Limited Focus on Non-Market Activities:**
Smith's theory primarily focuses on market transactions and the production of goods and services. Critics argue that this narrow focus neglects the significant contributions of non-market activities, such as unpaid work in households, volunteering, and community-based initiatives. These non-market activities contribute to societal well-being and economic development but are not adequately captured in Smith's theory.

4) **Incomplete Treatment of Institutions:**
Smith's theory emphasizes the importance of property rights and the rule of law for economic development. However, critics argue that his treatment of institutions is limited. Institutions, such as political systems, regulatory frameworks, and social norms, play a crucial role in shaping economic outcomes. Smith's theory does not provide a comprehensive framework for analyzing the role of institutions in economic development.

5) **Insufficient Consideration of Environmental Concerns:**
Critics argue that Smith's theory neglects environmental considerations and the potential negative externalities associated with economic development. The focus on economic growth and efficiency without proper consideration of environmental sustainability can lead to resource depletion, pollution, and ecological damage. Critics contend that a more holistic approach is needed to address the environmental challenges associated with economic development.

6) **Lack of Dynamics and Change:**
Smith's theory assumes a static economy with a focus on equilibrium outcomes. Critics argue that this perspective overlooks the dynamic nature of economic development and technological progress. Economic development involves structural changes, technological advancements, and shifts in production patterns over time. Smith's theory does not provide a robust framework for analyzing these dynamic processes.

7) **Limited Treatment of Global Interdependencies:**
Smith's theory primarily focuses on individual nations and their domestic economies. Critics argue that in today's interconnected world, economic development is influenced by global interdependencies, such as international trade, capital flows, and global institutions. Smith's theory does not adequately address the complexities of globalization and the challenges and opportunities it presents for economic development.

8) **Inadequate Treatment of Social and Cultural Factors:**
While Smith acknowledges the role of social institutions and cultural factors in economic development, critics argue that his theory does not provide a

comprehensive analysis of their impact. Social and cultural factors, such as social capital, trust, and cultural norms, can significantly shape economic outcomes. Critics contend that a deeper exploration of these factors is necessary for a more complete understanding of economic development.

4.2 Ricardo's Theory of Economic Development:

It appears that you are referring to David Ricardo, not Ricardo's Smith. David Ricardo was another influential economist who built upon and expanded upon many of Adam Smith's ideas. While Ricardo's work covered various aspects of economics, including trade and value theory, he also made significant contributions to the theory of economic development.

4.2.1 Key Elements of Ricardo's Theory:

Following are the key elements of Ricardo's theory of economic development.

1) **Comparative Advantage and International Trade:**

   One of Ricardo's most notable contributions is the concept of comparative advantage. He argued that countries should specialize in the production of goods or services in which they have a comparative advantage, meaning they can produce more efficiently relative to other goods or services. According to Ricardo, international trade based on comparative advantage benefits all participating countries, as it allows them to specialize and allocate resources more efficiently, leading to increased productivity and economic development.

2) **Population Growth and Agricultural Development:**

   Ricardo also discussed the relationship between population growth and agricultural development. He argued that as a country's population grows, the demand for agricultural products increases, leading to expansion in agricultural production. However, as more land is brought into cultivation, the diminishing returns to land eventually lead to reduced productivity. This phenomenon, known as the law of diminishing returns, implies that as population grows, a country must shift resources from agriculture to other sectors, such as manufacturing, to sustain economic development.

3) **Theory of Rent:**

   Ricardo developed the theory of rent, which explains the distribution of income in relation to land ownership. According to Ricardo, as population and demand for agricultural products increase, less fertile land must be cultivated, leading to higher rents for landowners. This theory of rent highlights the role of land as a factor of production and its impact on income distribution.

4) **Capital Accumulation and Industrial Development:**

   Ricardo recognized the importance of capital accumulation for industrial development and economic growth. He argued that a higher savings rate leads to increased investment and capital formation, which, in turn, fosters industrialization and economic development. Ricardo's theory emphasizes the role of capital accumulation in driving technological advancements, productivity gains, and the shift of resources from agriculture to industry.

5) **Labor Theory of Value:**
   Similar to Smith, Ricardo subscribed to the labor theory of value, which suggests that, the value of a good or service is determined by the amount of labor required for its production. This theory played a central role in Ricardo's analysis of economic development, particularly in relation to the distribution of income and profits.

6) **Critique of Malthusian Population Theory:**
   Ricardo engaged in a debate with Thomas Malthus on population growth and its impact on economic development. While Malthus argued that population growth would inevitably lead to resource scarcity and economic stagnation, Ricardo countered that technological progress and increased capital accumulation could mitigate the negative effects of population growth and promote economic development.

   It is important to note that Ricardo's theory of economic development was built upon the foundation laid by Adam Smith and further refined by subsequent economists. While his contributions were significant, his theories were not without criticism. For example, his labor theory of value has been subject to scrutiny and alternative theories of value have emerged. Nonetheless, Ricardo's work has played a crucial role in shaping the understanding of economic development and international trade, and his theories continue to be studied and debated by economists to this day.

4.2.2 Critics on Ricardo's Theory:

David Ricardo's theory of economic development, while highly influential in the field of economics has faced its share of criticisms. These criticisms stem from various aspects of his theory, including the labor theory of value, comparative advantage, assumptions about perfect competition, and the implications of his theory for income distribution.

1) **Labor Theory of Value:**
   One significant criticism of Ricardo's theory stems from his reliance on the labor theory of value. According to this theory, the value of a good or service is determined by the amount of labor required for its production. Critics argue that this theory fails to account for other factors that influence value, such as supply and demand dynamics, subjective preferences, and the role of capital and technology. Additionally, the labor theory of value does not adequately explain the pricing of services or intangible goods, leading to limitations in analyzing the full range of economic activities.

2) Assumptions of Perfect Competition:
Ricardo's theory is based on the assumption of perfect competition, where all firms and individuals have perfect information and operate in a market free from distortions. Critics argue that this assumption is unrealistic and fails to capture the complexities of real-world markets. Imperfections such as monopolies, market power, externalities, and information asymmetry are pervasive in actual economies and can significantly impact economic development outcomes. Neglecting these market imperfections limits the applicability of Ricardo's theory to real-world situations.

3) Oversimplification of Comparative Advantage:
Ricardo's theory of comparative advantage suggests that countries should specialize in producing goods or services in which they have a lower opportunity cost. While this theory provides a basis for international trade, critics argue that it oversimplifies the complexities of trade patterns. Factors such as economies of scale, transportation costs, technological differences, and government policies can influence trade patterns and render the assumptions of comparative advantage less applicable in certain situations.

4) Neglect of Institutional Factors:
Critics argue that Ricardo's theory does not adequately consider the role of institutions in economic development. Institutions, such as legal frameworks, property rights, political systems, and social norms, shape economic outcomes and influence the ability of countries to achieve sustained economic growth. Ricardo's theory focuses primarily on factors such as labor, capital, and technology, neglecting the critical role of institutions in creating an enabling environment for economic development.

5) Implications for Income Distribution:
Ricardo's theory has been criticized for its implications on income distribution. His theory suggests that as capital accumulates and industrialization progresses, profits increase at the expense of wages. This has led to concerns about the potential for widening income inequality and the concentration of wealth in the hands of a few. Critics argue that Ricardo's theory neglects the social and political consequences of unequal income distribution, which can hinder long-term economic development and social stability.

6) Lack of Dynamics and Change:
Ricardo's theory assumes a static economic framework and does not adequately address the dynamic nature of economic development. Critics argue that economic development involves structural changes, technological advancements, and shifts in production patterns over time. Ricardo's theory does not provide a comprehensive framework to analyze these dynamic processes, limiting its ability to explain the complexities of economic development in evolving economies.

7) **Environmental Considerations:**

Another criticism of Ricardo's theory is its limited consideration of environmental factors. Critics argue that his focus on economic growth and resource allocation fails to account for the potential negative externalities associated with economic development, such as environmental degradation, resource depletion, and climate change. This oversight raises concerns about the long-term sustainability of development patterns advocated by Ricardo's theory.

4.3 Malthus Theory of Economic Development:

Thomas Robert Malthus was an economist and demographer who proposed the Malthusian theory of economic development. His theory revolves around the relationship between population growth and resources, and it highlights the potential for population growth to outpace the availability of resources, leading to negative consequences for society.

4.3.1 Key Elements of Malthus Theory:

The key components of Malthus' theory of economic development are as follows:

1) **Population Growth:**

Malthus argued that population tends to grow exponentially, doubling over time, due to factors such as high birth rates and improved health and living conditions. He believed that population growth would eventually surpass the capacity of resources to sustain it.

2) **Resource Constraint:**

According to Malthus, resources, particularly food production, increase at a slower rate compared to population growth. He believed that there are inherent limits to resource availability, such as limited land for cultivation and finite natural resources.

3) **Diminishing Returns:**

Malthus posited that as population grows the productivity of agriculture and resource utilization faces diminishing returns. As more land is cultivated or resources are exploited, each additional unit of input produces diminishing marginal returns. This implies that the ability to increase production becomes constrained over time.

4) **Positive and Preventive Checks:**

Malthus proposed two types of checks on population growth. Positive checks refer to factors that reduce population through natural disasters, diseases, wars, and other calamities. Preventive checks, on the other hand, involve measures taken by society to limit population growth, such as delayed marriages, celibacy, and contraception.

5) **Misery and Poverty:**

Malthus argued that if left unchecked, population growth would lead to adverse social and economic consequences. As resources become scarce relative to the growing population, living standards would decline, leading to poverty, hunger, and general misery.

6) **Moral Restraint:**

Malthus advocated for moral restraint and personal responsibility in family planning as a means to control population growth. He believed that individuals and societies should exercise self-control in reproductive decisions to avoid the negative consequences associated with overpopulation.

7) **Policy Implications:**

Malthus' theory had significant policy implications. He argued against welfare programs and assistance to the poor, as he believed they would only encourage population growth and exacerbate the problem of resource scarcity. Instead, he emphasized the importance of personal responsibility and self-restraint in family planning.

4.3.2 Critics on Malthus Theory:

Malthus' theory of economic development has faced various criticisms over time. Some of the key criticisms include:

1) **Technological Progress:**

One major criticism is that Malthus did not adequately consider the potential for technological progress to increase resource availability and productivity. Technological advancements have historically played a crucial role in improving agricultural practices, resource extraction techniques, and overall productivity, thereby expanding the capacity to meet the needs of a growing population.

2) **Economic Growth and Structural Change:**

Malthus' theory largely overlooks the role of economic growth and structural change in shaping development outcomes. Economic growth, driven by factors such as investment, innovation, and market forces, can generate new resources, create employment opportunities, and improve living standards even with a growing population.

3) **Institutional Factors:**

Critics argue that Malthus did not sufficiently consider the impact of institutions on economic development. Institutions, such as property rights, governance structures, and social policies, play a crucial role in resource allocation, income distribution, and addressing issues of poverty and inequality. Neglecting the role of institutions can limit the explanatory power of Malthus' theory in understanding the complexities of economic development.

4) Global Perspective:
Malthus' theory tends to focus on local or national contexts and may not fully account for the global perspective of resource availability. While specific regions may face resource constraints, global trade, technological diffusion, and resource redistribution can alleviate local shortages and provide avenues for sustainable development.

5) Population Control Methods:
Malthus' advocacy for moral restraint and preventive checks has been criticized for its limited effectiveness and potential infringement on personal liberties. Critics argue that focusing solely on population control overlooks other policy measures, such as education, poverty reduction, and sustainable development, which can address the root causes of population growth and resource scarcity.

6) Social and Economic Dynamics:
Critics contend that Malthus' theory oversimplifies the social and economic dynamics of population growth and resource constraints. Factors such as changing consumption patterns, income distribution, and technological advancements can significantly influence resource utilization and availability.

7) Historical Evidence:
Critics argue that historical evidence does not fully support Malthus' dire predictions. While there have been instances of localized resource constraints and population-induced challenges, societies have demonstrated the ability to adapt, innovate, and find solutions to resource scarcity through technological advancements and social changes.

4.4 Karl Marx's Theory of Economic Development:

Karl Marx's theory of economic development, known as Marxist economics or Marxian economics, is a comprehensive framework that seeks to understand the dynamics of capitalist societies and their development over time. Grounded in historical materialism, Marx's theory examines the modes of production, class struggle, exploitation, and contradictions inherent in capitalist economies.

4.4.1 Key Elements of Karl Marx Theory:

Following are the key components of Marx's theory of economic development, their interconnections, and their implications.

1) Historical Materialism:
At the core of Marx's theory is historical materialism, which posits that the driving force of societal change is the material conditions of production. Marx argues that economic systems evolve in a dialectical process, with each stage of development characterized by specific relations of production and class struggle. Historical

materialism provides the framework for understanding the historical development and transformation of economies.

2) **Modes of Production:**

Marx identifies various modes of production throughout history, such as feudalism, capitalism, and socialism. A mode of production comprises the means of production (such as technology, tools, and machinery) and the relations of production (such as the social relations between owners of the means of production and the working class). Marx primarily focuses on the capitalist mode of production and its inherent contradictions.

3) **Capitalist Mode of Production:**

Marx's analysis centers on the capitalist mode of production, which is characterized by private ownership of the means of production, wage labor, and the pursuit of profit. In capitalism, capitalists (the bourgeoisie) own and control the means of production, while workers (the proletariat) sell their labor power to capitalists in exchange for wages. Marx emphasizes the exploitative nature of capitalism, where capitalists accumulate capital by extracting surplus value from workers.

4) **Exploitation and Class Struggle:**

Marx argues that capitalist societies are marked by the exploitation of labor. Capitalists profit by paying workers less than the value they produce through their labor, leading to surplus value appropriation. This exploitation creates a fundamental class conflict between the bourgeoisie and the proletariat. Marx sees class struggle as a driving force of historical change, with the working class ultimately seeking to overthrow the capitalist system.

5) **Contradictions of Capitalism:**

Marx identifies several contradictions within capitalism that he believes will lead to its eventual downfall. These contradictions include:

a) **Concentration of Wealth and Power:**

Marx highlights the tendency of capitalism to concentrate wealth and power in the hands of a few capitalists. Over time, competition and the pursuit of profit lead to the centralization and concentration of capital, creating monopolies and oligopolies that exploit workers and dominate markets.

b) **Exploitation and Alienation:**

Marx argues that the exploitation of labor in capitalism leads to the alienation of workers from their own labor. Workers are disconnected from the products of their work, leading to a sense of powerlessness and dehumanization.

c) **Tendency of the Rate of Profit to Decline:**

Marx observes a long-term tendency of the rate of profit to decline in capitalism. As capitalists seek to increase productivity through technological advancements and capital investment, the relative share of capital invested in machinery and technology increases, leading to a decline in the rate of profit.

d) Overproduction and Crises:

Marx argues that capitalism is prone to overproduction and economic crises. Capitalists, driven by the pursuit of profit, tend to produce more goods than can be consumed by the working class. This imbalance can lead to economic downturns, recessions, and periodic crises.

6) Transition to Socialism:

Marx envisions the transition from capitalism to socialism as the ultimate goal of his theory. In a socialist society, the means of production are owned collectively by the working class, and the profit motive and exploitation are eliminated. Marx believes that socialism would create a more equitable and just society, free from class antagonisms and exploitation.

4.4.2 Critics on Karl Marx Theory:

Critics of Marx's theory of economic development have raised several objections and criticisms. While Marx's work has had a significant impact on the field of economics and social theory, it is not without its detractors. Some of the key criticisms include:

1) Economic Calculation Problem:

One of the main criticisms of Marx's theory is related to the economic calculation problem in socialist economies. Critics argue that Marx's vision of a socialist society, where the means of production are collectively owned, lacks a mechanism for efficient allocation of resources. Without market prices and the profit motive, it becomes challenging to determine the relative value of goods and services, leading to inefficiencies and misallocation of resources.

2) Incentives and Innovation:

Critics contend that Marx's theory fails to adequately address the role of incentives in driving innovation and economic progress. By downplaying the significance of individual incentives and rewards, Marx's theory overlooks the role of entrepreneurship, innovation, and risk-taking in stimulating economic growth and development. Critics argue that without the prospect of individual gain and competition, there is a diminished motivation for individuals to take risks and innovate.

3) Ignoring Consumer Preferences:

Some critics argue that Marx's theory focuses too heavily on production and class struggle, neglecting the importance of consumer preferences and market dynamics. By disregarding the role of consumer demand and individual choices, Marx's theory fails to account for the diverse and evolving needs and preferences of individuals in society. Critics argue that understanding consumer demand and catering to it is essential for economic development.

4) Lack of Voluntary Exchange:

Marx's theory heavily critiques the capitalist system and the exchange of commodities through the market. However, critics argue that voluntary exchange, based on mutually beneficial transactions, is a key driver of economic development. They contend that the freedom to engage in voluntary exchange allows for specialization, efficiency, and the creation of wealth, leading to economic growth.

5) Lack of Individual Freedom:

Critics argue that Marx's theory undermines individual freedom and the right to private property. By advocating for the collective ownership of the means of production, Marx's theory limits individual autonomy and personal decision-making. Critics assert that individual freedom and property rights are crucial for fostering innovation, creativity, and entrepreneurship, which are vital for economic development.

6) Historical Determinism:

Another criticism of Marx's theory is its deterministic view of history. Critics argue that Marx's theory assumes a predetermined path of historical development, with capitalism inevitably leading to socialism. They contend that historical processes are complex and influenced by multiple factors, and the outcome is not predetermined. Critics assert that economic systems can evolve in various ways and that the transition to socialism is not necessarily an inevitable outcome.

7) Lack of Attention to Cultural and Institutional Factors:

Marx's theory predominantly focuses on economic factors and class struggle, often neglecting the significance of cultural and institutional factors. Critics argue that cultural values, norms, and institutions play a crucial role in shaping economic development. They contend that factors such as governance, rule of law, social norms, and cultural values can significantly impact economic outcomes and cannot be ignored in analyzing economic development.

4.5 Schumpeterian Theory of Economic Development:

The Schumpeterian theory of economic development, developed by the Austrian economist Joseph Schumpeter, provides a unique perspective on the process of economic growth and development. Schumpeter's theory emphasizes the role of innovation, entrepreneurship, and technological change as key drivers of economic progress.

4.5.1 Key Elements of Schumpeterian Theory:

Following are key components of the Schumpeterian theory of economic development:

1) Entrepreneurship and Innovation:

At the heart of Schumpeter's theory is the concept of entrepreneurship and innovation. Schumpeter believed that entrepreneurs play a crucial role in the economy by introducing new products, processes, and technologies. Innovation, according to Schumpeter, is the primary force that disrupts the existing economic order and leads to economic development.

2) **Creative Destruction:**
Schumpeter introduced the concept of "creative destruction," which refers to the process by which innovation and entrepreneurial activities replace outdated products, processes, and business models. Creative destruction involves the continuous cycle of new entrants challenging existing firms, leading to their decline or exit from the market. This process of creative destruction is seen as a driving force behind economic progress and growth.

3) **Entrepreneurial Profit:**
Schumpeter highlighted the role of entrepreneurial profit as a reward for successful innovation and risk-taking. Entrepreneurs who introduce new and improved products or technologies can earn above-average profits in the short run. These profits serve as an incentive for entrepreneurs to invest in innovation, leading to the dynamic development of the economy.

4) **Technological Change and Waves of Innovation:**
Schumpeter identified waves of innovation as significant drivers of economic development. These waves occur when clusters of innovations and technological advancements emerge in a particular industry or sector, leading to substantial changes in the economic landscape. These waves can have far-reaching effects on productivity, employment, and economic growth.

5) **Innovation and Business Cycles:**
Schumpeter's theory also acknowledges the connection between innovation and business cycles. He argued that waves of innovation can lead to fluctuations in economic activity, creating periods of expansion and contraction. Innovations can disrupt existing industries, leading to economic booms, followed by periods of economic downturn as the economy adjusts to the new technologies and market conditions.

6) **Role of Institutions:**
While Schumpeter's theory focuses primarily on the role of entrepreneurs and innovation, he also recognized the importance of supportive institutions for economic development. Institutions, such as intellectual property rights, legal frameworks, and financial systems, play a vital role in fostering entrepreneurship, protecting intellectual property, and facilitating the diffusion of innovations throughout the economy.

7) **Long-Run Dynamics:**
Schumpeter's theory emphasizes long-run dynamics and the cumulative impact of innovation on economic development. He argued that sustained economic growth is driven by the continuous introduction of new products, processes, and technologies.

Over time, these innovations create new industries, increase productivity, and lead to higher living standards.

4.5.2 Contributions of Schumpeterian Theory:

The Schumpeterian theory of economic development has made several important contributions to our understanding of economic progress:

1) **Emphasis on Innovation:**
Schumpeter's theory highlights the critical role of innovation in driving economic development. It recognizes that technological change and entrepreneurial activities are essential drivers of long-term economic growth.

2) **Entrepreneurial Spirit:**
The theory recognizes the importance of entrepreneurial behavior in the economy. Schumpeter's focus on entrepreneurs as agents of change highlights the significance of risk-taking, creativity, and resource allocation for economic development.

3) **Dynamic Perspective:**
The Schumpeterian theory provides a dynamic perspective on economic development. It acknowledges that economies are constantly evolving, driven by waves of innovation and creative destruction, rather than remaining in a static equilibrium.

4) **Link between Innovation and Business Cycles:**
The theory establishes a connection between innovation and business cycles, highlighting how technological advancements can drive economic expansions and contractions.

4.5.3 Critics on Schumpeterian Theory:

While the Schumpeterian theory of economic development has made significant contributions to our understanding of innovation and entrepreneurship, it has also faced criticisms from various perspectives. Some of the main criticisms include:

1) **Limited Scope of Innovation:**
Critics argue that the Schumpeterian theory focuses predominantly on technological innovations and neglects other forms of innovation, such as organizational innovations, social innovations, and incremental improvements. They argue that these forms of innovation are equally important for economic development and should not be overlooked.

2) **Uncertain Link between Innovation and Economic Growth:**
Critics contend that the direct link between innovation and economic growth is not always clear and straightforward. While innovation can drive growth in some cases, it does not always translate into widespread economic benefits. Factors such as

market conditions, regulatory environment, access to finance, and skills of the workforce can mediate the relationship between innovation and growth.

3) **Neglect of Demand-side Factors:**
The Schumpeterian theory tends to focus more on supply-side factors, such as technological advancements and entrepreneurial activities, while giving relatively less attention to demand-side factors. Critics argue that understanding consumer demand, market dynamics, and the interaction between supply and demand is crucial for sustainable economic development.

4) **Inequality and Concentration of Power:**
Some critics argue that the Schumpeterian theory can exacerbate income inequality and concentration of economic power. They contend that the disruptive nature of innovation and creative destruction can lead to job losses, market consolidation, and wealth accumulation in the hands of a few dominant firms or individuals, widening income disparities in society.

5) **Lack of Attention to Institutional Factors:**
Critics argue that the Schumpeterian theory underplays the role of institutional factors in shaping economic development. Institutions, such as property rights, rule of law, and regulatory frameworks, are crucial for creating an enabling environment for innovation, entrepreneurship, and investment. Neglecting these institutional factors can limit the effectiveness of innovation-driven economic development strategies.

6) **Ignoring Environmental Sustainability:**
Another criticism of the Schumpeterian theory is its limited consideration of environmental sustainability. Critics argue that the pursuit of constant innovation and economic growth can have negative environmental impacts, such as resource depletion, pollution, and climate change. They argue for the integration of sustainability considerations into economic development strategies.

7) **Lack of Policy Prescriptions:**
Some critics argue that the Schumpeterian theory provides limited guidance for policymakers in terms of specific policy interventions to promote innovation and economic development. They contend that the theory lacks concrete policy prescriptions and fails to address broader socio-economic challenges, such as poverty reduction, social inclusion, and equitable distribution of benefits.

Review Questions

Q. 1. Answer in 100 Words:

1) State the Contradictions of Capitalism.
2) Explain the Contributions of Schumpeterian Theory.

Q. 2. Answer in 200 Words:

1) Explain the Critics on Smith's Theory.
2) Discuss the Critics on Ricardo's Theory.
3) Explain the Critics on Karl Marx Theory.
4) State the Critics on Schumpeterian Theory.

Q. 3. Answer in 300 Words:

1) Explain the Key Elements of Smith's Theory.
2) Discuss the Key Elements of Ricardo's Theory.
3) Explain the Malthus Theory of Economic Development.
4) State the Key Elements of Karl Marx Theory.
5) Discuss the Key Elements of Schumpeterian Theory.

Q.4 Write Short Note on Following:

1) Key Elements of Malthus Theory.
2) Critics on Malthus Theory.
3) Karl Marx Theory.
4) Schumpeterian Theory.

❖❖❖❖❖❖❖

NOTES